THE EUCHARISTIC STORMS

Communion in the hand and marginalizing the Real Presence

Barry Forbes

With grateful and belated thanks to my parents (thanks, Mom!), who led me to Roman Catholicism with their conversion; to my beautiful wife, Linda, for all of her support; and, to our wonderful, large family, who have shown me what faith is really all about.

I also want to recognize the encouragement of a handful of reviewers who were critical to the mission of the book and helped keep me on track. I especially thank a learned, holy Roman Catholic priest who willingly shared his thoughts, ideas and enthusiasm for the project, but – because of his situation in Canada – must remain anonymous. Additionally, Louis Cruse, my daughter Jennifer, and, of course, Linda, were all very encouraging and helpful in too many ways to count. Christine Le Niles served as my copy editor, and her work was nothing less than masterful. Literally hundreds of people provided insightful articles to Communion-in-the-hand.org, and many of these articles served as background material for this book. I am most grateful to all of you.

Without all of your valued guidance and suggestions, this book wouldn't be the same.

Barry Forbes

ISBN: 1499374712
ISBN-13: 9781499374711
Library of Congress Control Number: 2014909343
CreateSpace Independent Publishing Platform
North Charleston, South Carolina

A NOTE FROM THE AUTHOR:

While researching *The Eucharistic Storms*, I catalogued a significant number of frequently accepted facts, figures, statements, quotations, and assumptions that turned out to be at least partially, and sometimes completely, untrue. Some were honest errors, others understandable misinterpretations of ancient passages. A few had taken on the status of urban legends, passed from one Internet site to another. In all cases, to the best of my ability, I have omitted anything that seemed questionable or was ultimately proven to be untrue. In a couple of cases, I have used specific quotations in order to show error, and I identified them as such in the text.

To some degree, this book is about *progressives* and *neo-modernists* and their impact on the Roman Catholic Church, its clergy and laity alike. These two terms are the most frequently used descriptions of post-Vatican II *modernists*. I use all three interchangeably throughout, as they are essentially one and the same.

Barry Forbes
May 16, 2014

INTRODUCTION

"This is the bread which came down from heaven, not such as the fathers ate and died; he who eats this bread will live for ever." This he said in the synagogue, as he taught at Capernaum. Many of his disciples, when they heard it, said, "This is a hard saying; who can listen to it?" John 6:58–60

Thus, an unknown number of His disciples walked away, never again to be seen in the Gospels. The first eucharistic storm—a storm, like all of its successors, of denial and disbelief—was born. Later in time, the day following the Last Supper, the storm grew sharply in intensity, quickly morphing into a deadly force of death and destruction.

For almost two millennia, the Roman Catholic Church and its faithful have been battered by eucharistic storms. A few arrived with gale-force winds that were recorded in time; others faded on landfall, so quickly that history failed to note their passing.

Three of the eucharistic storms were full-blown tsunamis that resulted in extensive, on-going carnage. Driven by violent persecutions, the first storm raged on for close to three centuries. The second major storm—birthed by Protestant reformers—has endured for close to half a millennium.

Yet the third massive eucharistic storm—now railing on for close to half a century—is arguably the most dangerous and destructive storm the Church has ever experienced. During its tenure, we have witnessed the greatest community mass desertion the world has ever seen. No one seems to have any idea how great the toll might be, but it is safe to say that well more than 100 million Catholics worldwide walked away; analogous to a handful of Christ's early disciples, the vast majority of these people will never be seen again. This is spiritual suicide on an unimaginable scale, negatively impacting every culture, race, religion, and nation, whether realized or not.

The greatest example of this institutionalized folly is irreverent Communion in the hand, the highly visible symbol of a deadly eucharistic storm.

CONTENTS

PROLOGUE

"I am the bread of life. Your fathers ate the manna in the wilderness, and they died. This is the bread which comes down from heaven, that a man may eat of it and not die. I am the living bread which came down from heaven; if any one eats of this bread, he will live for ever; and the bread which I shall give for the life of the world is my flesh." The Jews then disputed among themselves, saying, "How can this man give us his flesh to eat?" So Jesus said to them, "Truly, truly, I say to you, unless you eat the flesh of the Son of man and drink his blood, you have no life in you; he who eats my flesh and drinks my blood has eternal life, and I will raise him up at the last day. For my flesh is food indeed, and my blood is drink indeed. He who eats my flesh and drinks my blood abides in me, and I in him. As the living Father sent me, and I live because of the Father, so he who eats me will live because of me. This is the bread which came down from heaven, not such as the fathers ate and died; he who eats this bread will live for ever." This he said in the synagogue, as he taught at Capernaum. Many of his disciples, when they heard it, said, "This is a hard saying; who can listen to it?" But Jesus, knowing in himself that his disciples murmured at it, said to them, "Do you take offense at this? Then what if you were to see the Son of man ascending where he was before? It is the spirit that gives life, the flesh is of no avail; the words that I have spoken to you are spirit and life. But there are some of you that do not believe." For Jesus knew from the first who those were that did not believe, and who it was that would betray him. John 6:48–64

CHAPTER ONE

The Visible Language of Adoration

In 1829, the terrible Irish persecutions—borne so long and bravely by faithful Irish Catholics—finally began to wane into a painful national memory. The British Parliament had passed the Catholic Emancipation Act.

Over the previous 250 years, Irish Catholics had suffered horribly, their lands and lives stripped from them in a never-ending frenzy of anti-Catholicism, often in circumstances gruesome beyond words. Priests and bishops were hunted like wild animals with prices on their heads; faithful Catholics who harbored them were hanged at their front doors. Thousands paid the ultimate price.

Oliver Cromwell, under whom life was never pleasant, enacted the *Oath of Abjuration* in 1643, then reissued an even more objectionable form in 1656. Everyone was to be "adjudged a Papist" who refused the oath, condensed into a few formulas against the Catholic tenets:

> I, NAME, abhor, detest, and abjure at the authority of the Pope, as well in regard of the Church in general, as in regard of myself in particular. I condemn and anathematize the tenet that any reward is due to good works. I firmly believe and avow that no reverence is due to the Virgin Mary, or to any other saint in heaven; and that no petition or adoration can be addressed to them without idolatry. I assert that no worship or reverence is due to the sacrament of the Lord's Supper, or to the elements of bread and wine after consecration, by whomsoever that consecration may be made. I believe there is no purgatory, but that it is a popish invention; so is also the

> tenet that the Pope can grant indulgences. I also firmly believe that neither the Pope, nor any other priest can remit sins, as the papists rave. And all this I swear. . . .[1]

Cromwell devised the oath that, by Act of Parliament, every Irish Catholic was compelled to take. Threats, fines, imprisonment, banishment, and death were all employed to pervert the people's faith. The consequent penalties for refusing to take the hated oath began with the confiscation of two-thirds of the recusant's goods, to be repeated every time they refused. Additionally, anyone who spurned the oath was deprived of virtually every civic right. This, it was thought, would conquer the obstinacy of the gentry, who would soon be reduced to penury, and of the poor, who might easily be shipped to Barbados. (Apparently, 17,000 faithful were indeed so banished.)[2]

Yet no matter what the Edwardian Protestants forced on them, the vast majority of Irish people rejected Protestantism, and refused to abandon their Catholic faith.

The British finally acknowledged reality: With the passing of the Emancipation Act, they effectively admitted that the Irish would never surrender their love for the Real Presence of God Himself, profoundly expressed in their Roman Catholic faith.

Over time, this eucharistic storm slowly faded into history. Irish Catholics would once again practice their faith without fear of retribution.

Charles Forbes René, the Count of Montalembert, a loyal and acclaimed Catholic son of a French nobleman and an English mother, toured Ireland just months later, writing in his memoirs: "I will never forget the first mass which I heard in a country chapel. I rode to the foot of a hill, the lower part which was clothed with a thick plantation of oak and fir, and alighted from my horse to ascend it. I had taken only a few steps on my way when my attention was attracted by the appearance of a man who knelt at the foot of one of the firs; several others became visible in the same attitude; and the higher I ascended the larger became the number of these kneeling peasants. At length, on reaching the top of the hill, I saw a cruciform building, badly built of stone, without cement and covered with thatch. Around it knelt a crowd of robust and vigorous men, all uncovered, though the rain fell in torrents and the mud quivered beneath them. Profound silence reigned everywhere... I reached the door at the moment of elevation, and all of this pious assembly had prostrated themselves with their faces on the earth." [3]

A few years later, British soldiers, patrolling on horseback in rural Ireland, came on an astonishing sight. As they slowly ambled past Irish farm workers, laboring in the fields on the outskirts of a village, church bells began to peal in the distance. Suddenly, the workers dropped their farm implements to the ground and fell on their knees.

Facing a village Catholic church that could be heard but not seen, the Irish made the sign of the cross, silently prayed for a few minutes, then picked their implements up and returned to work. They had knelt knowing that something wondrous was happening: The pealing of the village church bells indicated that the Host—the Real Presence, the Body, Blood, Soul, and Divinity of Christ Himself—had just been elevated at Mass in the sacred act of consecration.

Possibly, the soldiers had never seen anything like it. British memories were sanitized almost three hundred years earlier with the eradication of transubstantiation, an ambiguous redefinition of the Real Presence, and the severance of ties to apostolic succession. Ever since, Anglican (Episcopalian), and other Protestant denominations interpreted Christ's presence at the celebration of the Lord's Supper to be either only spiritual, or symbolic, or non-existent. Perhaps the soldiers believed they had witnessed nothing more than one of many "Romish superstitions," happily jettisoned by sixteenth-century reformers.

Yet perhaps for just one or two of the soldiers, the scene might have been inspirational beyond words.[4]

The visible language of adoration appears throughout all of recorded history. We find its inspiring truth and beauty in the Old and the New

Testament, in the scrolls and writings of the Early Church Fathers, and in the great spiritual works of saints and scholars that have survived antiquity. Invariably, each of us is called to kneel and adore in His presence, for God Himself deserves nothing less.

God made certain that we would know what was expected of us; without doubt, it is an obligation of each of us to respond accordingly.

Long before the birth of Jesus Christ, the teaching was very clear in the Old Testament:

> O come, let us worship and bow down, let us kneel before the LORD, our Maker. (Psalm 95:6)

> Turn to me and be saved, all the ends of the earth! For I am God, and there is no other. By myself I have sworn, from my mouth has gone forth in righteousness a word that shall not return: "To me every knee shall bow, every tongue shall swear." (Isaiah 45:22–23)

> And at the evening sacrifice I rose from my fasting, with my garments and my mantle rent, and fell upon my knees and spread out my hands to the LORD my God. (Ezra 9:5)

> When Daniel knew that the document had been signed, he went to his house where he had windows in his upper chamber open toward Jerusalem; and he got down upon his knees three times a day and prayed and gave thanks before his God, as he had done previously. (Daniel 6:10)

> Solomon had made a bronze platform five cubits long, five cubits wide, and three cubits high, and had set it in the court; and he stood upon it. Then he knelt upon his knees in the presence of all the assembly of Israel, and spread forth his hands toward heaven; and said, "O LORD, God of Israel, there is no God like thee, in heaven or on earth,

> keeping covenant and showing steadfast love to thy servants who walk before thee with all their heart. (2 Chronicles 6:13–14)

Repeatedly in the New Testament, we are instructed to kneel and adore in the presence of God:

> [T]hey beckoned to their partners in the other boat to come and help them. And they came and filled both the boats, so that they began to sink. But when Simon Peter saw it, he fell down at Jesus' knees, saying, "Depart from me, for I am a sinful man, O Lord." (Luke 5:7–8)

> Jesus heard that they had cast him out, and having found him he said, "Do you believe in the Son of man?" He answered, "And who is he, sir, that I may believe in him?" Jesus said to him, "You have seen him, and it is he who speaks to you." He said, "Lord, I believe"; and he worshipped him. (John 9:35–38)

> In all things I have shown you that by so toiling one must help the weak, remembering the words of the Lord Jesus, how he said, 'It is more blessed to give than to receive.'" And when he had spoken thus, he knelt down and prayed with them all. (Acts 20:35–36)

> And I heard every creature in heaven and on earth and under the earth and in the sea, and all therein, saying, "To him who sits upon the throne and to the Lamb be blessing and honor and glory and might for ever and ever!" And the four living creatures said, "Amen!" and the elders fell down and worshiped. (Revelation 5:13–14)

> And he came out, and went, as was his custom, to the Mount of Olives; and the disciples followed him. And when he came to the place he said to them, "Pray that you may not enter into

> temptation." And he withdrew from them about a stone's throw, and knelt down and prayed, "Father, if thou art willing, remove this cup from me; nevertheless not my will, but thine, be done." (Luke 22:39–42)

Even Christ Himself, while praying to the Father, fell on His knees.

Thirty-three years earlier, around the time when Jesus was born in Bethlehem of Judah, the three wise men—known today as the Magi—witnessed an unusual nighttime phenomenon in the eastern skies: An incredibly bright star, one that no one could possibly fail to observe, lit up the heavens. The Magi's prophets knew what the star portended, for this wonder had been foretold long before: It was the announcement of the birth of a new king, one destined to be unlike any other, who someday would rule the entire world.

The skyward phenomenon eventually became known as the Star of Bethlehem.

In a search for this wondrous newborn child, the Magi embarked on a long and dangerous journey, crossing multiple borders into unknown territories. In time, the star led them into the land ruled by King Herod:

> "Where is he who has been born king of the Jews? For we have seen his star in the East, and have come to worship him." When Herod the king heard this, he was troubled, and all Jerusalem with him; and assembling all the chief priests and scribes of the people, he inquired of them where the Christ was to be born. They told him, "In Bethlehem of Judea; for so it is written by the prophet: 'And you, O Bethlehem, in the land of Judah, are by no means least among the rulers of Judah; for from you shall come a ruler who will govern my people Israel.'" Then Herod summoned the wise men secretly and ascertained from them what time the star appeared; and he sent them to Bethlehem, saying, "Go and search diligently for the child, and when you have found him bring me word, that I too may come and worship him." When they had heard the king they went their way;

> and lo, the star which they had seen in the East went before them, till it came to rest over the place where the child was. When they saw the star, they rejoiced exceedingly with great joy; and going into the house they saw the child with Mary his mother, and they fell down and worshipped him. Then, opening their treasures, they offered him gifts, gold and frankincense and myrrh. (Matthew 2:2–11)

Three centuries later, St. John Chrysostom (347–407 AD), recognized by both the Eastern Orthodox Church and the Latin Church as a saint and Doctor of the Church, fully understood the message of the Magi, and what it meant for each of us:

> This Body, even lying in a manger, Magi reverenced. Yea, men profane and barbarous, leaving their country and their home, both set out on a long journey, and when they came, with fear and great trembling, worshipped Him. Let us, then, at least imitate those Barbarians, we who are citizens of heaven.[5]

Theodore the Interpreter (ca. 350–428), bishop of Mopsuestia (modern Yakapinar) from 392 to 428 AD, captured the essence of the sacrificial Christ about to nourish anticipatory souls with the Sacred Species:

> It is the deacons who bring out this oblation . . . which they arrange and place on the awe-inspiring altar, a vision . . . awe-inspiring even to the onlookers. By means of the symbols we must see Christ, who is now being led out and going forth to his passion, and who, in another moment, is laid out for us on the altar. . . . And when the offering that is about to be presented is brought out in the sacred vessels, the patens and chalices, you must think that Christ the Lord is coming out, led to his passion . . . by the invisible host of ministers . . . who were also present when the passion of salvation was being accomplished.[6]

In his church, the assembled adorers would then be on their knees.

Many centuries later, in 1916, a year of preparation for Our Lady's presence at Fatima, the Angel of Peace appeared three times to Lucia, Jacinta, and Francisco. Sister Lucia's account of the final apparition, which occurred either at the end of the summer or the beginning of autumn, is riveting:

> [W]hile the children were grazing their sheep at the Cabeco again, the angel suddenly appeared to them a third time. Through the white radiance of his presence the children could see that he held a chalice with a Host above it, from which drops of Blood fell into the cup. Leaving these suspended in mid-air, he prostrated himself before them and repeated the following sublime prayer of reparation three times in the same tone of trembling fervor.
>
> "Most Holy Trinity, Father, Son, and Holy Ghost, I adore Thee profoundly. I offer Thee the most precious Body, Blood, Soul, and Divinity of Our Lord Jesus Christ, really and truly present in every tabernacle of the world in reparation for the countless outrages, sacrileges, and indifferences by which He is offended. And through the infinite merits of His Most Sacred Heart and of the Immaculate Heart of Mary, I beg Thee to convert poor sinners."
>
> The angel then gave the Host to Lucia and the chalice to Francisco and Jacinta to drink from. He then prostrated himself once more on the ground and repeated the above prayer three times very slowly with the children before disappearing from their ecstatic gaze.[7]

An angel, a pure spirit, who lives constantly in the intimate presence of God, had prostrated himself before the Eucharist in adoration. For young Francisco, it was such an overwhelming experience that he spent the balance of his short years trying to console his Savior. Every moment he could, he spent in front of the Blessed Sacrament, attempting to atone in some small manner for the indifferent way that people respond to the Bread of Life.

Almost a century later, over the final five years of his pontificate, Pope Benedict XVI distributed Communion only on the tongue, and only to those who knelt.[8] (There were a handful of well-publicized exceptions to this rule, none of which were ever explained by Rome.) Benedict, too, fully understood the visible language of adoration, and what it meant. In his book *The Spirit of the Liturgy*, Cardinal Joseph Ratzinger, the future Pope Benedict XVI, wrote decisively about kneeling before God: "Communion only reaches its true depth when it is supported and surrounded by adoration."[9]

For this reason, Cardinal Ratzinger maintained that "the practice of kneeling for Holy Communion has in its favor a centuries-old tradition, and it is a particularly expressive sign of adoration, completely appropriate in light of the true, real and substantial presence of Our Lord Jesus Christ under the consecrated species."[10]

Kneeling comes from the Bible and its knowledge of God. Benedict wrote about *proskynein*, which describes an attitude towards submission or worship, especially of prostrating oneself before God: "[T]he word *proskynein* alone occurs fifty-nine times in the New Testament, twenty-four of which are in the Apocalypse, the book of the heavenly liturgy, which is presented to the Church as the standard for her own liturgy."[11]

If one does not kneel before the Lord, when does one kneel? "[T]he man who learns to believe learns also to kneel, and a faith or a liturgy no longer familiar with kneeling would be sick at the core."[12]

In a widely read interview, Vatican liturgist Monsignor Guido Marini said the Pope was attempting to set the stage for the whole Church as to the proper norm for receiving Communion: "Kneeling highlights the truth of the Real Presence in the Eucharist, helps the devotion of the faithful, and introduces the sense of mystery more easily."[13]

Kneeling is the ultimate posture of adoration, submission, and surrender. In the Roman Catholic Church, we fall to our knees during Mass and humbly adore Him . . . just as St. Paul instructed us (Ephesians 3:14). We genuflect and kneel to indicate, by bodily attitude, a total submission of our minds and hearts to the true presence of Our Lord Jesus Christ. It is an exterior manifestation of the reverence inspired by His Real Presence, necessary before and after receiving the eucharistic Christ.

A celebrated saying of St. Augustine (354–430 AD), Doctor of the Church and one of the most revered Early Church theologians, teaches us well:

> Christ took earth from earth, inasmuch flesh is from earth, and this flesh he took from the flesh of Mary; and because he conversed with us in the flesh, he gave us this same flesh to eat for our salvation. . . . But no one eats that flesh without adoring it first; not only is it no sin to adore it, but we sin if we adore it not.[14]

God is present. Adoration, veneration, and reverence are not options, but happy obligations.

In our Roman Catholic liturgy, the visible language of adoration in the Real Presence of God (the Eucharist) grew organically, and was slowly but surely codified into the eucharistic practice. Cardinal Antonio Canizares Llovera, prefect for the Vatican's Congregation for Divine Worship and the Discipline of the Sacraments, encouraged Catholics to consider receiving Holy Communion on the tongue as a "sign of adoration that needs to be recovered."[15]

In response to an interview in December 2008, Cardinal Llovera talked about how we should receive the Holy Eucharist:

> What does it mean to receive Communion in the mouth? What does it mean to kneel before the Most Holy Sacrament? What does it mean to kneel during the consecration at Mass? It means adoration,

> it means recognizing the real presence of Jesus Christ in the Eucharist; it means respect and an attitude of faith of a man who prostrates before God because he knows that everything comes from Him, and we feel speechless, dumbfounded, before the wondrousness, his goodness, and his mercy. That is why it is not the same to place the hand, and to receive communion in any fashion, than doing it in a respectful way; it is not the same to receive communion kneeling or standing up, because all these signs indicate a profound meaning.[16]

To receive the Eucharist on our tongue, Cardinal Llovera said, "is to signify our humility before the Lord and to recognize that it is God himself who feeds us." When we do so, we "know that we are before God himself and that he came to us and that we are undeserving."[17]

Thus, these exalted words of praise and thanksgiving from great spiritual teachers seek to restore that which was so carelessly lost, much of it willingly swept away in a fifty-year frenzy of "renewal" and innovation. At countless churches around the globe, a eucharistic storm—engendered by the enemy within—wrought unprecedented, on-going destruction to the Church and its faithful.

Now, after almost five decades of "renewal" and "transformation", one must wonder:

If Jesus knelt before His Father in prayer, should we not kneel to receive God Himself in the Real Presence? Was the heavenly example of pure adoration shown by the Angel of Peace, together with his prayerful gift for all of Catholicism, nothing more than a nice legend to be ignored at will? Was Fatima, a Vatican-approved apparition, just a quaint fable? What about the Magi, the Early Church Fathers, all the revered saints, plus the great spiritual leaders of antiquity and today? What about the Bible?

Were they all wrong?

1 Patrick Francis Moran, *Historical Sketch of the Persecutions Suffered by the Catholics of Ireland Under the Rule of Oliver Cromwell* (Dublin: Callan, 1903), ch. 8, sec. 2.

2 Father Thomas J. McGovern, *The Most Holy Eucharist* (Manchester, NH: Sophia Institute Press, 2013), 225–74.
3 M .O .W. Oliphant, *Memoir of Count De Montalembert,* (Edinburg and London, William Blackwood and Sons, 1872), 98
4 Based on Irish legend.
5 Philip Schaff, *Nicene and Post-Nicene Fathers: First Series, Vol XII: St. Chrysostom: Homilies on the Epistles of Paul to the Corinthians* (New York: Cosimo Classics, 2007), 143.
6 Hugh Wybrew, *The Development of the Eucharistic Liturgy in the Byzantine Rite* (Crestwood, NY: St. Vladimir's Seminary Press, 1989), 53.
7 Francis Johnston, *Fatima: The Great Sign* (Charlotte, NC: Tan Books, 1980), 25.
8 The exceptions to this rule have been published on hundreds of websites *ad infinitum.*
9 Joseph Ratzinger, *The Spirit of the Liturgy* (San Francisco: Ignatius Press, 2000), 90.
10 Office for the Liturgical Celebrations of the Supreme Pontiff, "Communion Received on the Tongue and While Kneeling," http://www.vatican.va/news_services/liturgy/details/ns_lit_doc_20091117_comunione_en.html.
11 Ratzinger, *Spirit of the Liturgy*, 80.
12 Ibid., 185–94.
13 *L'Osservatore Romano*, June 26, 2008.
14 Cumming, John and Daniel French, *The Hammersmith Protestant Discussion* (London: Arthur Hall, Virtue & Co., 1852), 40.
15 James D. Conley, "The Manner of Receiving Holy Communion," *Catholic News Agency*, http://www.catholicnewsagency.com/resources/roman-missal-3rd-edition/bishops/the-manner-of-receiving-holy-communion.
16 See http://en.wikipedia.org/wiki/Antonio_Ca%C3%B1izares_Llovera.
17 Ibid.

CHAPTER TWO

No Communion, No Survival

In 1945, Gregory Dix, an Anglican monk who lived during the first half of the twentieth century, roiled his brotherhood with the release of the classic, controversial Early Christian book *The Shape of the Liturgy*.[1] During three hundred years of sometimes savage persecutions, he wrote, "The storm center throughout the entire period was undoubtedly the Eucharist."[2]

It was, in fact, the Christians' worship of the Bread of Life after transubstantiation—the changing of the elements of the bread and wine, when they are consecrated in the Eucharist, into the Body and Blood of Christ, the Real Presence—that generated deep, irrational distrust. A turbulent obsession of suspicion came not just from the general population, but from neighbors, friends, and even family members. Dix noted,

> When we regard what actually took place in the early eucharistic rite, the fear and hatred it inspired over so long a time seems ridiculous. Yet it is an uncanny fact that there is scarcely any subject on which the imagination of those outside the faith is more apt to surrender to the unrestrained nonsense of panic than that of what happens at the catholic eucharist.[3]

Where did this panic originate? In the strange, new cult of Christianity, people worshiped an unknown God Whose Body they ate and Blood they drank. They were accused of being cannibals who held secret, forbidden meetings. They converted others to their mysterious creed, and dunked them in the river. They espoused radically different, life-changing beliefs often at odds with the existing culture, and they lived accordingly, sometimes distinctly apart from mainstream society. Thus, it became relatively common and easy to disdain, scorn, and even hate Christians, especially with encouragement from the governing levels of society.

The state had its own officially approved worship; there was no room for a nascent, unrecognized interloper. In the eyes of pagan rulers, the worship of the Eucharist constituted a dangerous crime.

Nonetheless, despite all odds, the vast majority of Early Christians refused to surrender their faith, a treasure which was unified around the wondrous gift that Christians celebrated among themselves: the Holy Eucharist. It was Christ in the Real Presence that provoked the first eucharistic storm, a deadly offensive that would tyrannize Christians across three blood-soaked centuries. Somewhere around 20,000 faithful paid the ultimate price for their love and adoration.

Why? What possessed so many to stand so firmly, even unto death itself?

Early Christians recognized, embraced, and practiced an essential truth that many of us today were never taught, have long forgotten, or perhaps hadn't ever accepted. Josef A. Jungmann, S.J., one of the great liturgists of the twentieth century, captured its essence while quoting the martyrs of Abitinae during the Diocletian persecution: "We cannot survive without the Eucharist. The eucharistic celebration cannot be superseded."[4]

Early Christians firmly believed that there is no life without the Blessed Sacrament nor without the celebration to confect the eucharistic elements of bread and wine into the Body and Blood of Christ. They had certainly studied and embraced the Psalms, particularly Psalm 62, with its compelling line, "For your love is better than life."

Jungmann penned that, at the beginning of the second century, "the name for the celebration of the Mass generally found in the Greek writers is *Eucharistia.*" Ignatius of Antioch uses this name. So does the *Didache*, not only in the prayers but also in a passage where express mention is made of the Sunday service: "On the Lord's day meet and break bread and the Eucharist, after having first confessed your offenses, so that your sacrifice may be pure."[5]

Jungmann added: "Here the old term *to break bread* is employed side by side with the new term *Eucharistia* or *thanksgiving* [I]n order that we may be enabled to give God due thanks, Christ gave us *the bread of the Eucharist.*"[6]

From Origen we read: "[B]ut to God who has bestowed upon us an abundance of benefits . . . we fear being ungrateful. The sign of this gratitude towards God is the bread called Eucharist."[7]

In 155 AD, St. Justin Martyr wrote to Emperor Antoninus to explain what Christians did during their rituals. Christians were being persecuted for their "atrocities" and the saint was appealing for reason:

> On the day we call the day of the sun, all who dwell in the city or country gather in the same place. The memoirs of the apostles and the writings of the prophets are read, as much as time permits. When the reader has finished, he who presides over those gathered admonishes and challenges them to imitate these beautiful things. Then we all rise together and offer prayers for ourselves . . . and for all others, wherever they may be, so that we may be found righteous by our life and actions, and faithful to the commandments, so as to obtain eternal salvation. When the prayers are concluded we exchange the kiss.
>
> Then someone brings bread and a cup of water and wine mixed together to him who presides over the brethren.
>
> He takes them and offers praise and glory to the Father of the universe, through the name of the Son and of the Holy Spirit and for a considerable time he gives thanks (in Greek: eucharistein) that we have been judged worthy of these gifts.

> When he has concluded the prayers and thanksgivings, all present give voice to an acclamation by saying: "Amen."[8]

Every thinking Christian was well aware of the penalty for worshiping the Bread of Life, yet they came in ever-increasing numbers. Christians embraced the Eucharist as the purest form of thanksgiving, and reverence in the manner of reception was axiomatic. The Sacred Feast was strictly reserved for baptized believers: "Allow no one to eat or drink of your Eucharist, unless they have been baptized in the name of the Lord. For concerning this, the Lord has said, 'Do not give what is holy to dogs.'"[9]

The faithful washed the palms of their hands before receiving the consecrated Bread. Communicants bowed earnestly, receiving the Body of the Lord into the mouth directly from the right hand, and not from the left. Their fingers never touched the Host. The palm of the hand served as a kind of paten or corporal, especially for women, who wore a cloth known as a *dominica* over their hands. Thus, one reads in a sermon of St. Caesarius of Arles (470–542): "When they desire to communicate, all men wash their hands, and all women show their splendid garments when they receive the Body of Christ."[10]

Customarily, the palm of the hand was purified or washed after the reception of the eucharistic Bread, as is still the norm for the Communion of clerics in the Byzantine Rite.

Large basins were placed by the doors to the church, or the room where the Eucharist was to be celebrated. Propriety demanded that hands be scrupulously clean, for communicants would receive the Eucharist on their palms. There was also another higher reason for the washing: that of symbolizing freedom from all stain of sin. Certainly, the hand that touched the Blessed Sacrament was to be clean physically, and the soul spiritually. The washing of hands symbolized the internal purification from all that stained body and soul.[11]

In the Clementine Liturgy (Antioch) of the fourth century, there were groups within the assembly that were barred from taking part in the Eucharist. These groups were dismissed individually, prior to distribution, and prayed for as they departed. They included catechumens being prepared for baptism, energumens believed to be possessed by unclean spirits, illuminati in the final stages of preparation for initiation, and penitents excluded from Communion while they did penance for grave sin. Not only could they not receive Him, they were deemed unworthy to be in His presence.[12]

Similarly, in Constantinople at the time of St. John Chrysostom (AD 347–407), catechumens were first prayed for and dismissed, followed by penitents. (The latter certainly formed a recognizable group, for Chrysostom remarked that people were more ashamed of being recognized as sinners than of having committed the sin itself!)[13]

Saint Ephraim was one of the great authors of the Syrian Church. Because of his beautiful writings, he is sometimes referred to as the "lyre of the Holy Spirit." In AD 338, he aspired to the diaconate and remained a deacon for the remainder of his life. He wrote:

> Our Lord Jesus took in His hands what in the beginning was only bread; and He blessed it, and signed it, and made it holy in the name of the Father and in the name of the Spirit; and He broke it and in His gracious kindness He distributed it to all His disciples one by one. He called the Bread His living Body, and did Himself fill it with Himself and the Spirit.
>
> And extending His hand, He gave them the Bread which His right hand had made holy: "Take, all of you, eat of this; which My word has made holy. Do not now regard as bread that which I have given you; but take, eat this Bread, and do not scatter the crumbs; for what I have called My Body, that it is indeed. One particle from its crumbs is able to sanctify thousands and thousands, and is sufficient to afford life to those who eat of it. Take, eat, entertaining no doubt of faith, because this is My Body, and whoever eats it in belief eats in it Fire and Spirit. But if any doubter eat of it, for him

> it will be only bread. And whoever eats in belief the Bread made holy in My name, if he be pure, he will be preserved in his purity; and if he be a sinner, he will be forgiven." But if anyone despise it or reject it or treat it with ignominy, it may be taken as certainty that he treats with ignominy the Son, who called it and actually made it to be His Body."[14]

The Most Rev. Juan Rodolfo Laise captured early reverence and beauty in his work *Communion in the Hand: Documents and History.* He wrote about the Nestorians, separated completely since the end of the fifth century, not only from Rome but also from Antioch and Byzantium. The Nestorians represent the oldest schismatic group that still exists. All of their ancient practices have been preserved, including reception only at Christmas and Easter, as well as the actual form of reception.[15]

A Western witness is quoted—a Dominican missionary to Mosul, who visited the Nestorians around 1890 and wrote of his experience in detail:

> All come up seriously and with recollection. At the entrance to the Sanctuary, on the Epistle side, there is a smoking censer. Each communicant, in passing it, incenses his hands, his face and his breast with it, then, upon arriving before the priest, he remains upon foot, kisses his hand and presents his right palm extended and crossed over the left hand. The priest places there a particle of the Host, which the communicant immediately consumes by licking his palm, which he then passes over his forehead to wipe it; after that he goes before the subdeacon, kisses the sleeve of his alb, drinks from the chalice, wipes his mouth with the purificator and then withdraws to the Gospel side, keeping his hand over his lips. The women communicate the same way, but at the end of the Mass, after the men have left. . . . I was impressed by the orderliness and recollection that visibly prevailed in this ceremony.[16]

In the first few centuries, then, every thoughtful communicant would know that he or she was receiving something, and Someone, very special. Accordingly, adoration, veneration, and reverence were expected and due, and the cleansing of body and soul was an unconditional prerequisite to reception.

Following the twentieth-century "re-introduction" of Communion in the hand, we often heard that the Church was merely "reviving" an ancient Catholic tradition. That claim was misleading at best. Instead, those words were merely the early warning for a new, breaking eucharistic storm of denial and disbelief, the opening of an epic torrent that has yet to run its course. For today's Communion in the hand is a close derivative of the communion service from the Protestant Reformation, specifically designed to repudiate the Catholic dogma of transubstantiation and the Real Presence (see Chapter Six). Clearly, it cannot be compared with the life-transforming, reverent Communion in the hand practiced, at various times, in the first few centuries.

By the standards of the Early Church, the commonality of today's irreverence is stunning. Standing and receiving in the hand is merely symptomatic. The sacrificial fasting of the communicant is minimal at best; reception while in a state of serious sin is reportedly common; any recognition of the Real Presence is often marginal or non-existent; disbelief in the eucharistic God is rampant; adoration, veneration, and reverence are, for many, unknown, unwelcome, or wholly absent; and Extraordinary Ministers of Holy Communion (EMHCs) often distribute the Bread of Life unnecessarily, despite clear instructions from Rome.

While those distributing the Eucharist have certainly seen many communicants piously receive the Lord on the hands, they also regularly see the opposite: people rarely make the required external sign of reverence before receiving; few make a throne with their hands to receive the Lord, even after decades of admittedly weak catechesis; many try to receive with dirty hands, gloves, or with their fingers; and some walk away without ingesting the Sacred Host.

Worse, Communion in the hand makes it pitifully easy to steal a Host for foolish or even sacrilegious purposes. Priests, deacons, and eucharistic ministers also note the abject inconsistency between piously purifying fingers and vessels of any eucharistic particles for those distributing Communion, while similar requirements are non-existent for those who receive such particles, together with Sacred Hosts, in their hands.

Distribution of the Blessed Sacrament in such a disconnected, casual, and irreverent manner places the Holy Eucharist at grave risk. There is often little or no emphasis on Catholic faithful receiving worthily, a core Christian belief spanning two millennia. To whatever degree humanly possible, the Church is gravely obligated to protect the Bread of Life from those who would receive unworthily, and to discourage those in a state of mortal sin and non-believers from offending God through reception. That obligation is shared by every Roman Catholic, from the pope, to his priests, and to the laity.

Quite obviously, kneeling to receive on the tongue sends a deeply resonant message that, in its absence, has encouraged denial, disbelief, confusion, and indifferentism.

A major barometer of today's irreverence is the collapse of the sacrament of confession, one of the more unfortunate after-effects of Vatican II. As confessions dropped precipitously, the percentage of Sunday communicants increased dramatically. Apparently, too few of us were, or are, willing to give any consideration to the inspired wisdom of St. Paul:

> For as often as you eat this bread and drink the cup, you proclaim the Lord's death until he comes. Whoever, therefore, eats the bread or drinks the cup of the Lord in an unworthy manner will be guilty of profaning the body and blood of the Lord. Let a man examine himself, and so eat of the bread and drink of the cup. For any one who eats and drinks without discerning the body eats and drinks judgment upon himself. That is why many of you are weak and ill, and some have died. (1 Corinthians 11:26–30)

The irrefutable fact is that each of us has a moral obligation to receive God worthily. To do otherwise is betrayal.

No matter how one considers it, the systemic refusal to protect the Blessed Sacrament is nothing less than catastrophic failure. Today's unfortunate manner of reception has caused irreparable harm, aiding and abetting the loss of millions of souls who deserted the faith.[17]As shocking as this reality is, it shouldn't be: Polls show that a significant percentage of Roman Catholics no longer believe in the Real Presence.[18] To one degree or another, this denial is the fruit of irreverent Communion in the hand while standing, and receiving from an EMHC who often shouldn't be there.

Certainly, people have deserted the faith for myriad reasons; yet in the final analysis, millions walked away because they refused to believe, or had never been taught, that the Roman Catholic Church is the anointed custodian of transubstantiation and the Real Presence, the one and only custodian in the singular Church of the Holy Eucharist. There is no other.

Deep in the center of a virtually silent eucharistic storm now bearing down on half a century, a momentous number of former Catholics deserted the Church without ever hearing those words spoken from the pulpit.

That is a tragedy beyond words.

1 Gregory Dix, *The Shape of the Liturgy*, 2nd ed. (Westminster: Dacre Press, 1945), 141–55.

2 Ibid., 145. Fifteen hundred years later, this theme was central to the Protestant Reformation, and today, 500 years after that, new battle lines are once again being formed around the Eucharist.

3 Ibid.,145.

4 Josef A. Jungmann, S.J., *The Early Liturgy, To the Time of Gregory the Great* (Notre Dame, IN: University of Notre Dame Press, 1959), 13.

5 *The Didache*, XIV, http://thedidache.com.

6 Jungmann, *The Early Liturgy*, 39–44.

7 Origen, *Contra Celsum*, VIII, 57, in *Patrologia Graeco-Latina*, ed. Jacques-Paul Migne, vol. 11 (Paris: Garnier Fratres, 1857–64), 1601ff.

8 *Catechism of the Catholic Church*, no. 1345, http://www.usccb.org/beliefs-and-teachings/what-we-believe/catechism/catechism-of-the-catholic-church/epub/index.cfm#.

9 *The Didache*, X.

10 Mary Magdeleine Mueller, OSF, trans., *The Fathers of the Church: St. Caesarius*, Vol. 66 (Washington, DC: Catholic University of America Press, 2004), 167.

11 Casimir Kucharek, *The Byzantine-Slav Liturgy of St John Chrysostom* (Allendale, NJ: Alleluia Press, 1973), 248–49.

12 Rather than offering an *Our Father* or three *Hail Mary*'s, penance for serious sin could take *years* to expiate.

13 Hugh Wybrew, *The Orthodox Liturgy* (Yonkers, NY: St. Vladimer's Seminary Press, 1996), 39–51.

14 Pasquini, John J., *True Christianity: The Catholic Way* (Bloomington, IN: iUniverse, 2003), 318–19.

15 Juan Rodolfo Laise, *Communion in the Hand: Documents and History* (Boonville, NY: Preserving Christian Publications, 1997).

16 Attributed to E. Tisserant, "L'Eglise nestorienne," *Dictionnaire de la theologie catholique,* t. XI, col. 315, in Laise, *Communion in the Hand, Documents and History*.

17 Even potential converts can be confused. Mainline Protestants would instantly recognize the "symbolism" of the Catholic Communion service, a close duplicate of what was created in the sixteenth-century Protestant Reformation, but would also fail to realize or acknowledge the Real Presence of God Himself in the Sacred Host.

18 Mary Gautier, "Knowledge and Belief About the Real Presence," *National Catholic Reporter*, October 2011, http://ncronline.org/news/catholics-america/knowledge-and-belief-about-real-presence.

CHAPTER THREE

Expanding the Base

A couple of years ago, an afternoon talk show host on Catholic radio accepted a call from a concerned listener. A younger woman, sounding to be perhaps in her early twenties, was calling to express her doubts about receiving Communion in the hand.

"I've never been comfortable with the idea," she said. "Somehow it just doesn't seem right to me. What exactly does the Church teach?"

The program host assured his listener, together with a worldwide audience, that Communion in the hand was perfectly fine, and that, in fact, the Catholic Church encouraged it. This had been, he stated, a common practice throughout the first millennium. As proof of the Church's vision, he quoted what every apologist of Communion in the hand falls back on, reciting a few lines generally attributed to St. Cyril, Bishop of Jerusalem and Doctor of the Church, from the fourth century:

> In approaching, therefore, come not with thy wrists extended, or thy fingers spread; but make thy left hand a throne for the right, as for that which is to receive a King. And having hollowed thy palm, receive the Body of Christ, saying over it, *Amen*. So then after having carefully hallowed thine eyes by the touch of the Holy Body, partake of it; giving heed lest thou lose any portion thereof; for whatever thou losest, is evidently a loss to thee as it were from one of thine own members.[1]

This is a beautiful, convincing verse, which goes a long way to explain why we hear it so often. Yet, until the 1969 "re-introduction" of Communion in the hand, the average lay person had rarely, if ever, heard of this reading. That changed quickly.

Very little is known about St. Cyril's early years. It is believed he was born at or near Jerusalem between AD 310 and 315, and that he received an excellent literary education. He was ordained a priest by Bishop Maximus, and appointed a bishop in AD 348 by Acacius of Caesarea. In the famous twenty-first oration of St. Gregory Nazianzen, the author speaks of Acacius being "the tongue of the Arians."[2]

When Maximus died, Cyril was consecrated bishop of Jerusalem. Because he was supported by Acacius, the Arian bishop of Caesarea, the orthodox criticized the appointment; at the same time, the Arians thought they had gained a friend. Both factions were wrong, as Cyril carefully navigated a middle road between the two.

Nonetheless, Cyril soon found himself engulfed in the battle over Arianism. The schism had sprung up in the third century, and raged throughout most of the fourth century. Arianism taught that God the Father and the Son did not exist together eternally, and that the pre-incarnate Jesus was a divine being created by, and therefore inferior to, God the Father. Arians believed that, at some point, the Son did not exist.

One way or another, Arianism touched most church members—from simple believers, priests, and monks, to bishops and even members of Rome's imperial family.

Soon after his consecration, a conflict arose between Cyril and Acacius, and the Arians began to attack the bishop of Jerusalem as the confessor and defender of the Nicene faith. The initial cause of the falling out was territory, not beliefs. As bishop of Caesarea, Acacia had authority over all the bishops of Palestine. Cyril argued that this authority did not include Jerusalem because Jerusalem was an "apostolic see"—one of the original sees set up by the apostles. When Cyril refused to appear at councils called by Acacius, the Arian bishop accused Cyril of selling church goods to raise money. Consequently, the emperor sided with Acacius and banished Cyril.[3]

For various reasons, Cyril was expelled from his see three times within the course of approximately twenty years, the last time being the longest, at eleven years. It was only in AD 378 that Cyril could definitively resume possession of his see, and restore unity and peace to the faithful.[4]

After his death, Cyril was not often cited, but gradually, as knowledge of his theology spread throughout the centuries, his major writings were embraced by theologians around the world. In 1893, he was proclaimed a Doctor of the Church by Pope Leo XIII. His feast is celebrated in both the Eastern and the Western church on March 18th.

Saint Cyril is credited with twenty-four catechetical lectures, considered to be one of the most precious treasures of Christian antiquity. The lectures fall within two groups: The first group includes an introductory discourse and eighteen *Catecheses.* These were addressed to an audience that consisted principally of those who had, prior to Lent, elected to receive Christian initiation through baptism by total immersion, chrism, and Holy Communion. This would occur during the night of Holy Saturday, and the early morning of Easter Sunday. (Excepting an emergency, adult baptism was the rule in the fourth century.)

These *Catecheses* are classic theological documents, containing an exceptionally clear and well-argued presentation of the main points of the Catholic faith. They seem to have been spoken *ex tempore* and written down at some later time, probably by what we would consider today to be nuns or monks. The year is almost certainly AD 350.

The second group is known as the five *Mystagogical Catecheses,* instructions addressed to the neophytes during Easter week. These instructions are based on the liturgical ceremonies of the three sacraments received by the neophytes during the Easter Vigil. The first two (19–20) deal with baptism; the third (21) with confirmation; the fourth (22) with eucharistic doctrine; and the fifth (23) with the Liturgy of the Mass.

Today, the quotation attributed to Cyril—"In approaching, therefore, come not with thy wrists extended, or thy fingers spread; but make thy left hand a throne for the right"—is taken directly from the eucharistic oration. This is the single verse routinely deployed to justify and propagate today's irreverent Communion in the hand; it is not the only quotation, but assuredly the most common one. Sixteen hundred years after Cyril's death, his words have become famous.

When reciting this verse, the Catholic radio host was far from alone. Yet rarely will an apologist for Communion in the hand ever mention that there has been deep and lasting debate as to whether or not Cyril is actually the author of the five *Mystagogical Catecheses.*

One of the myriad discussions in print appeared in the 1950 series *Patrology: The Golden Age of Greek Patristic Literature.* The author, Johannes Quasten, pointed to multiple scholars, writers, and theologians (Schermann, Swaans, Richard, Telfer, and others) who attribute the five *Mystagogical Catecheses* to Cyril's successor, a presumed Arian named John.

At the same time, Quasten wrote that others believed it possible that something similar to these instructions *was* delivered by Cyril, then later written—and revised, with discrepancies in style—again, perhaps by John. Additionally, there are existing documents in which the introductory discourse and eighteen *Catecheses* are presented, but the five *Mystagogical Catecheses* never appear.[5] Thus, some scholars believe the five instructions were simply added by an unknown writer around fifty years later.[6]

Others have noted that Arians could have been promoting Communion in the hand as a sign of their disbelief in the divinity of Jesus Christ. Based on the times and the power that Arianism wielded, this could be a convincing theory; however, the reverential tone of the verse makes this assertion somewhat implausible.

Absent any new evidence, the debate about the five *Mystagogical Catecheses* won't be resolved anytime soon.

For knowledgeable progressives, there is no advantage to be gained by admitting controversy and doubt. For similar reasons, the very next reading in the same eucharistic oration is rarely mentioned. In fact, it is usually avoided like the plague:

> Then after thou hast partaken of the Body of Christ, draw near also to the Cup of His Blood; not stretching forth thine hands, but bending and saying with an air of worship and reverence, *Amen*, hallow thyself by partaking also of the Blood of Christ. And while the moisture is still upon thy lips, touch it with thine hands, and hallow thine eyes and brow and the other organs of sense. Then wait for the prayer, and give thanks unto God, who hath accounted thee worthy of so great mysteries.[7]

In essence, this reading is asking us to smear the blood of Christ on our eyes and ears to protect us from the Evil One. Saint Cyril of Alexandria compared the smearing of the sensory organs with the Blood of the Lamb immolated in the Eucharist to the smearing of the doorposts of the captive Jews in Egypt with the blood of a slaughtered lamb.[8] Just as this practice protected the Jews, so the smearing of the sensory organs would prevent the destructive evil of sensory temptation entering through them.[9]

Did anything like this really occur? It appears so: Jungmann and others believed it did, although this would certainly seem discordant with the veneration due to the Sacred Species; moreover, anything similar could be labeled abusive and even superstitious. If this was indeed a practice of the Early Church in the first few centuries, it faded away for obvious reasons. Still, the practice of actually *kissing* the Host became widespread. Theodoret, Bishop of Cyrrhus in Syria, confirmed that the excess of kissing the Host was already in use in the first half of the fifth century: "One should consider how during the sacred mysteries we take the limbs of the Spouse, kiss them, embrace them and apply them to our eyes."[10]

This practice—made possible by reception in the hand, thereby opening the door to abuse—persisted at least down to the end of the eighth century at one church or another. Saint John of Damascus (675–749) wrote: "Let us receive the Body of the crucified, and applying it to our eyes, our lips, and forehead, let us partake of the Divine burning coal."[11]

Progressives love to quote the eucharistic oration, verse xxi ("make thy left hand a throne"), but never mention the following verse xxii ("and hallow thine eyes and brow and the other organs of sense"). However, many theologians believe *both* verses led to abuses which the Church, in time, decisively corrected. Accordingly, no matter who wrote them, it is evident that the *Mystagogical Catecheses* cannot be authentically employed to excuse or promote either of these two practices, one of which is, at a minimum, weird and even superstitious.

Most specifically, exploiting a questionable reading—the author quite possibly unknown, and the subject ultimately banned—in order to promote today's irreverent Communion in the hand cannot be justified under any circumstances.

Most of us intrinsically understand and appreciate what reverence is and what it signifies. In today's Roman Catholic Church, walking up to God Himself and standing to receive Him in the hand never made sense, any more than it would have to dip one's fingers into His Sacred Blood and smear it into the sensory organs. Even in the early centuries of the first millennium, it appears that reverent Communion in the hand evolved into a serious problem that the Church was forced to address, then abandon.

Had reverence endured, it is doubtful that Communion in the hand would have been banned—but it was.

A few hundred years passed before the ban was accepted at every far-flung church, but the ruling prevailed across fourteen centuries. It wasn't until the pontificate of Paul VI that the door was opened to an innovative and decidedly irreverent manner of reception.

From the dawning of Christianity, the Church has been forced to cope with one eucharistic storm or another and, occasionally, concurrent storms. The target, always, is the Real Presence, God Himself, in the Holy Eucharist. If we surrender to this present storm, if we fail to rekindle deep reverence and love for the Blessed Sacrament, we lose everything—for the Early Christians, it turns out, had it right:

Without the Holy Eucharist—without an unshakeable belief in the Real Presence, for which an estimated 20,000 Early Christians surrendered their lives—there is no survival.

1 St. Cyril, *Catechesis Mystagogica* V, xxi–xxii, in *Patrologia Graeco-Latina*, ed. Jacques-Paul Migne, 33 (Paris: Garnier Fratres, 1857–64).
2 St. Gregory Nazianzen, *Oration*, xxi, 21, http://www.newadvent.org/fathers/310221.htm.
3 See "St. Cyril of Jerusalem," http://www.catholic.org/saints/saint.php?saint_id=40.
4 *Benedict XVI*, General Audience, June 27, 2007.
5 Johannes Quasten, *Patrology: The Golden Age of Greek Patristic Literature*, vol. III (Notre Dame, IN: Ave Maria Press, 1950), 363–67.
6 William Telfer, *Cyril of Jerusalem and Nemesius of Emesa* (Louisville, KY: Westminster John Knox Press, 1955), 38–39.
7 Cyril of Jerusalem, *Catechesis mystagogica* V, xxii, in Migne, *Patrologia Graeca*, 33.
8 Michael Davies, *Pope Paul's New Mass* (Kansas City, MO: Angelus Press, 1980), 457.
9 Theodoret of Cyrrhus, *Canticum Canticorum interpretatio*, I, 1, in Migne, *Patrologia Graeca*, 81, col. 27ff.
10 Ibid.
11 St. John of Damascus, *De fide Orthodoxa IV*, 13, in Migne, Patrologia Graeca, 94, col. 1149b.

CHAPTER FOUR

From Christ to the Seventh Century

One of Christianity's most dramatic historical scenes plays itself out vividly in St. John's Gospel: "Jesus answered, 'It is he to whom I shall give this morsel when I have dipped it.' So when he had dipped the morsel, he gave it to Judas, the son of Simon Iscariot" (John 13:26).

At the Last Supper, when Christ changed ordinary bread and wine into His Body and Blood, a claim often made is that the Bread of Life was placed directly into the hands of the apostles, including Judas. However, a traditional custom of Middle-Eastern hospitality during the time of Jesus, and even today, is that one feeds his guests symbolically from one's own hand. The first morsel is placed in the mouth of each guest: "Then after the morsel, Satan entered into him. Jesus said to him, 'What you are going to do, do quickly'" (John 13:27).

Then Judas betrayed Jesus, selling Him off for thirty pieces of silver.

Did Our Lord place the wet Bread of Life into Judas' hand? One could only imagine how messy that would have been. The thousands of paintings, drawings, and lithographs produced throughout the centuries depict this scene many ways, with the apostles receiving on the tongue or in the hand, sitting, standing, kneeling, or, commonly, lying back on giant sofas or pillows. However, each work of art is uniquely a product of the artist's imagination; no one really knows. (Interestingly enough, Communion in the hand reportedly never appears in any art that has survived the first six hundred years of Christianity.)

In point of fact, there is no written record that specifically defines the manner of reception, and that includes the Gospels. Still, it would have been most unusual, and very much out of character, for Jesus to spurn a traditional custom of His time.[1]

Moreover, long before the Last Supper, even prior to the time of Christ, we were introduced to the symbolism of receiving as a child, and in the mouth:

> "But you, son of man, hear what I say to you; be not rebellious like that rebellious house; open your mouth, and eat what I give you." And when I looked, behold, a hand was stretched out to me, and, lo, a written scroll was in it; and he spread it before me; and it had writing on the front and on the back, and there were written on it words of lamentation and mourning and woe. (Ezekiel 2:8–10)

> And he said to me, "Son of man, eat what is offered to you; eat this scroll, and go, speak to the house of Israel." So I opened my mouth, and he gave me the scroll to eat. And he said to me, "Son of man, eat this scroll that I give you and fill your stomach with it." Then I ate it; and it was in my mouth as sweet as honey. (Ezekiel 3:1–3)

Although receiving the Eucharist from the hands of Our Lord Jesus Christ would have been extraordinary beyond anything one could imagine, receiving in the mouth would not have been unusual or unexpected. Either way, on the tongue or in the hand, Christ's unveiling of the Holy Eucharist infused us with the miraculous hope of forgiveness and salvation. At the same time, the Last Supper, whence we received this greatest gift, emerged as the opening act of a continuing debate over the proper reception of the Bread of Life.

We can't prove the manner of reception at the Last Supper, but one thing is certain: Somewhere, at specific times, for reasons we can only surmise, reverent Communion in the hand was allowed by the Church.

It is often claimed that Communion in the hand was the normal practice throughout the first millennium. This assertion is clearly erroneous. Prior to around AD 150, there is almost nothing but historical silence. Later, the evidence—elusive, sketchy, frequently debatable, yet definitely conclusive—ebbs and flows sporadically throughout the ages, sometimes emerging from the mysterious pages of time as just a sentence or two. Then it disappears again, for years and even decades, before surfacing once more.

However, a case can definitely be made in which reverent Communion in the hand was, in all probability, common—although not necessarily exclusive—at times during the first five or six centuries. Then, over the next few hundred years, it was driven into oblivion, beginning around the turn of the century in AD 600.

The Last Supper was the prelude to the crucifixion of Our Lord and Savior. On His death, the first eucharistic storm, alive and seething since Capharnaum, spilled out into the streets. The persecutions began in earnest, Christian blood flowed, and tyranny commenced a three hundred-year reign.

Christ's twelve apostles led the way. Although Judas Iscariot killed himself, of the eleven remaining apostles, only one—John the Apostle, the son of Zebedee and the younger brother of the Apostle James—died from natural causes in exile. The other ten apostles were reportedly martyred by various means, including beheading by sword and spear and, in the case of Peter, crucifixion upside down.

Persecutions always threatened, but came and went erratically. One never knew when the next peril might suddenly appear, and what form it might take. Christians were well aware that their faith could be tested and the ultimate sacrifice required – at a moment's notice.

In Josef A. Jungmann's work, we learn just how threatening and tenacious the pagan culture could be:

> The first enemy was the pagan state which tried, in ever renewed attacks, to repress Christianity by force and violence. From Nero to Diocletian, the persecutions continued, now gentle, now harsh, their persistence as well as their ferocity highlighting the

> apparent antinomy between Christendom and the pagan Empire. The seeming paradox in the development of Christianity is that it took place in spite of the opposition of the Roman government, and the paradox is made all the greater by the attitude of the Christians themselves, who offered absolutely no resistance to persecution.[2]

The adversary was often legion in scope. The first documented case of imperially supervised Christian persecution occurred in the Roman Empire in AD 64. A great fire broke out in Rome, destroying portions of the city and economically devastating the Roman population. The Emperor Nero himself was suspected to be the arsonist, accused of playing the lyre and singing the *Sack of Ilium* during the fires. Nero made sure, however, that the strange Christian sect was blamed for the fire, and it was Christians who paid the price. From Roman historian Tacitus, obviously a non-Christian, in his AD 116 work *Annals*:

> Consequently, to get rid of the report, Nero fastened the guilt and inflicted the most exquisite tortures on a class hated for their abominations, called Christians by the populace. Christus, from whom the name had its origin, suffered the extreme penalty during the reign of Tiberius at the hands of one of our procurators, Pontius Pilatus, and a most mischievous superstition, thus checked for the moment, again broke out not only in Judæa, the first source of the evil, but even in Rome, where all things hideous and shameful from every part of the world find their centre and become popular. Accordingly, an arrest was first made of all who pleaded guilty; then, upon their information, an immense multitude was convicted, not so much of the crime of firing the city, as of hatred against mankind.[3]

In *The City of God,* written early in the fifth century, St. Augustine of Hippo summed it up visually: "The martyrs were bound, imprisoned, scourged, racked, burnt, rent, butchered—and they multiplied."[4]

State-sponsored distrust and outright hate easily incited the people at a moment's notice. By the mid-second century, mobs could be found willing to throw stones at Christians, and occasionally they could be mobilized by rival sects. The persecution in Lyon, for example, was preceded by mob violence, including assaults, robberies, and stonings.[5]

Further state persecutions were desultory until the third century. The first documentable empire-wide persecution took place under Maximinus Thrax, though only the clergy was targeted. It was not until the mid-century, under Decius, that a persecution of Christian laity across the empire took place. Decius authorized roving commissions, visiting cities and villages to supervise the execution of the sacrifices and to deliver written certificates to all citizens who performed them. Christians either fled to safe havens in the countryside, or faced the consequences.

Father John Zuhlsdorf, in an article titled *Communion in the Hand and the Threat of Death*, documented the story of Tarcisius, a famous Early Church martyr:

> Tarcisius was a boy of third-century Rome. His virtue and devotion were so strong that the clergy trusted him to bring the Blessed Sacrament to the sick. Once, while carrying a pyx, he was recognized and set upon by a pagan mob. They flung themselves upon him, trying to pry the pyx from his hands. They wanted more than anything to profane the Sacrament. Tarcisius' biographer, the fourth-century Pope Damasus, compared them to a pack of rabid dogs. Tarcisius "preferred to give up his life rather than yield up the Body of Christ." Even at such an early age, Tarcisius was aware of the stakes. Jesus had died for love of Tarcisius. Tarcisius did not hesitate to die for love of Jesus.[6]

The final persecution of the Early Church lasted until Constantine I came to power in AD 313 and legalized Christianity. The Emperor issued the so-called Edict of Toleration at Milan, granting full freedom of religion and worship. He also ordered the restitution of all Church property and places of worship. Later in the fourth century, Christianity would become the official religion of the empire under Theodosius I.

During earlier times of terror, the consecration of the bread and wine into the Body and Blood of Jesus Christ was held secretly, usually in fear, and often quite infrequently. Holy Communion was the Bread that unified and inspired Christian believers, shared by loyal followers with their families and loved ones, in a valiant effort to thank God and keep the faith alive.

Was the Eucharist received in the hand by persecuted Christians? If there was a transition, is this when Communion in the hand was introduced? We don't know, and we probably never will; the vast majority of documentary evidence appears beginning early in the third century. Prior to AD 150, all the way back to AD 33, it is all but dark, with a couple of notable exceptions.

A transition to Communion in the hand sometime therein is a common theory, and it is certainly possible. In a fierce eucharistic storm driven by violent and deadly persecutions, this could make sense: Communion in the hand would protect both the Eucharist *and* communicants by shrouding reception, and enable the common practice of covertly taking the Bread of Life home, or to other communicants, for another day. However, a transition is merely a theory and, to date, impossible to prove.

Advocates of Communion on the tongue frequently point to St. Basil of Caesarea (AD 329/330–379) and his oft-quoted verse to prove that, during times of persecution, Communion in the hand was allowed as an exception to the rule:

> If one feels he should in times of persecution, in the absence of a priest or deacon, receive Communion by his own hand, there should be no need to point out that this certainly shows no grave immoderation; for long custom allows this in such cases. In fact, all solitaries in the desert, where there is no priest, reserving Communion in their dwellings, receive It from their own hands.[7]

Although St. Basil's words appear to show an exception to Communion on the tongue, the same reading ends with this declaration, demonstrating that Communion in the hand was normal and customary for his time:

> And even in the church, when the priest gives the portion, the recipient takes it with complete power over it, and so lifts it to his lips with his own hand. It has the same validity whether one portion or several portions are received from the priest at the same time.[8]

A century later, Pope St. Leo the Great (ca. AD 400–461), considered one of the greatest popes ever, was leading the Church during the collapse of the Roman Empire. Notably, Saint Leo read the sixth chapter of St. John's Gospel as referring to the Eucharist (as all the Church Fathers did). In a preserved sermon on John 6, Saint Leo says: *Hoc enim ore sumitur quod fide creditur* (Serm. 91.3) ("This indeed is received by means of the mouth which we believe by means of faith").

The mouth is the means by which the Holy Eucharist is received, but the quotation is surely ambiguous. No matter how one accepts the Bread of Life, in the hand or on the tongue, one receives in the mouth. This quotation can be interpreted either way.

Alternatively, Fr. Casimir Kucharek—a brilliant priest, scholar, and writer who was fluent, or had reading knowledge, in twelve languages—documented the customary practice of receiving Communion in the hand in the ancient persecuted Church.[9] In *The Sacramental Mysteries: A Byzantine Approach*, he noted the following:

- Origen (d. AD 253/254): "When you receive the body of the Lord, you do it with all caution and reverence so that not even the tiniest particle of it falls to the ground, so that not a bit of the consecrated gift be lost."
- Dionysius of Alexandria (d. AD 265): Speaks of the same practice as a partaking of Christ's body and blood when he tells of

a man who doubted the validity of his baptism though he "has stood at the holy table, has stretched forth his hand to receive the holy food, and had been a partaker of the body and blood of our Lord Jesus Christ for a very long time."

- Tertuillian (d. AD 222): Writes of the same custom when he bewails the reception of idol-makers into the Church and the fact that they "would apply to the Lord's body those same hands which fashion bodies on demons."
- Kucharek says Christ's words recorded in Matthew 18:8 should be taken literally: "What hands should be cut off quicker than those in which scandal is done to the Lord's body?"

Another revered priest, scholar, and writer, Father Adrian Fortescue, earned a triple doctorate, including a rare Doctor of Divinity, over his short, deeply inspiring life. In the early part of the twentieth century, he was considered perhaps the most outstanding scholar among the clergy of the English-speaking world. (Reportedly, he was so fluent in ten different languages that he could lecture in any one of them!)

In his 1913 epic work *The Mass: A Study in the Roman Liturgy*, Fortescue confirmed that there were many Early Church witnesses documenting "that the Host was put into the hand of the communicant." He also studied Origen at length and the Early Church times he lived in, writing "Communion was of course given under both kinds; the consecrated bread was taken in the hand and sometimes carried home for Communion."[10]

Seemingly, the end to persecutions had little or no known impact on the manner of reception; reverent Communion in the hand continued unabated for another three centuries, and apparently long after, in different far-flung churches. There was, however, one documented change that emerged a few decades later, ending the practice noted above by Fortescue, that had flourished for at least a couple hundred years. Saint Justin Martyr also referred to the practice in his letter to Emperor Antoninus in AD 155: "When he who presides has given thanks and the people have responded, those whom we call deacons give to those present the 'eucharisted' bread, wine and water and take them to those who are absent."[11]

From the *Catholic Encyclopedia* of 1913:

> In the early days of the Church the faithful frequently carried the Blessed Eucharist with them to their homes . . . or upon long journeys . . . , while the deacons were accustomed to take the Blessed Sacrament to those who did not attend Divine service . . . as well as to the martyrs, the incarcerated, and the infirm.[12]

With the cessation of persecutions, permission for a lay person to carry the Eucharist home for other family members, or for another day, was withdrawn. It is believed there was no longer a need to place the Bread of Life at risk, thereby eliminating a major opportunity for abuse.

The Council at Saragozza, held in AD 380, wasn't shy about it. Anyone who failed to consume the Eucharist at Mass would be punished with excommunication:[13] "If someone is proved not to have consumed the grace of the Eucharist received in church, let that one be anathema in perpetuity. By all the bishops it was said: It is agreed."[14]

The Council of Toledo, AD 400, found it necessary to decree that whoever receives the Eucharist and does not eat it should be considered sacrilegious.[15] Thus, there is no doubt whatsoever that during the three centuries of persecution, and at least two or three centuries after, Communion was received in the hand—not exclusively, but most assuredly in the hand at one church or another and, it seems, quite commonly. No one knows if this manner of reception began as a result of the persecutions, with the original practice being Communion on the tongue. We simply have no witnesses and no documented proof.

The on-going debate over the manner of reception in the Early Church—on the tongue or in the hand, how, when, and where—is, therefore, unlikely ever to be resolved.

It is also superfluous to a much larger and far more important historical picture.

1 As others have pointed out, however, it is also important to remember that the apostles were themselves priests, or even bishops. Most of us are not and should not be handling the Holy Eucharist except in extraordinary circumstances.
2 Jungmann, *The Early Liturgy*, 109–10.
3 See http://en.m.wikipedia.org/wiki/Tacitus_on_Christ.
4 St. Augustine, *The City of God*, XXII, 6.
5 Eusebius, *Ecclesiastical History* 5.1.7.
6 Father John Zuhlsdorf, "Communion in the Hand and the Threat of Death," *Fr. Z's Blog*, http://wdtprs.com/blog/2006/06/communion-in-the-hand-and-the-threat-of-death.
7 However, one should remember he wrote *after* the persecutions had concluded. What happened one or two centuries earlier could easily have been shrouded in time, even in St. Basil's day.
8 M. J. Rouët de Journel, *Enchiridion Patristicum* (Barcelona: Editorial Herder, 1956), no. 916.
9 Casimir Kucharek, *The Sacramental Mysteries: A Byzantine Approach* (Allendale, NJ: Alleluia Press, 1976), 164–65.
10 Adrian Fortescue, *The Mass: A Study in the Roman Liturgy* (Fitzwilliam, NH: Loreto, 2012), 30–34.
11 *Catechism of the Catholic Church*, no. 1345, http://www.usccb.org/beliefs-and-teachings/what-we-believe/catechism/catechism-of-the-catholic-church/epub/index.cfm#.
12 "The Real Presence of Christ in the Eucharist," *The Catholic Encyclopedia*, http://www.newadvent.org/cathen/05573a.htm.
13 Some scholars believe this rule was nothing more than a means of forcing people to "take the chalice" while they were in attendance. However, the definitive threat of excommunication seems to indicate a far more serious problem was being addressed.
14 Virginia Burrus, *The Making of a Heretic: Gender, Authority, and the Priscillianist Controversy* (Berkeley, CA: University of California Press, 1995), 36–37.
15 Josef A. Jungmann, *The Mass of the Roman Rite: Its Origins and Development* (New York: Benziger Brothers, 1951), 381. Note that councils didn't write the rules for the universal Church, but history demonstrates that the Church frequently followed them.

CHAPTER FIVE.

From the Seventh Century to the Middle Ages

Sometime in the sixth century, the manner of receiving the Bread of Life passed through an emblematic transition. Father Adrian Fortescue documented the historical shift: "It seems that as early as the time of St. Gregory I (AD 590–604) it was sometimes put into the mouth, as now."[1]

Half a century later, shortly after the time of St. Gregory I, in AD 650, the Synod of Rouen delivered this instruction to the faithful, codifying Communion on the tongue into their eucharistic practice:[2]

> It has been reported to us that priests after saying Mass while they themselves consume the Divine Mysteries, hand over the chalice of the Lord to women who have made offerings for their Masses, or to some lay persons who cannot discern the Body of the Lord. . . . The piety of the faithful understands how contrary all this is to every ecclesiastical religion. Therefore we enjoin on all priests that no one in future presumes to act in this manner, but that the priest himself consumes the Eucharist with reverence and then hands it to the deacon or subdeacon who minister at the altar for distribution. . . .
>
> A priest should not put the holy Eucharist into the hands of any lay person or woman, but only into their mouths. . . .
>
> If any one will transgress this, because he despises almighty God and dishonors what belongs to God, let him be removed from the altar.[3]

Four decades on, in AD 692, the Synod of Trullo appeared to reverse course:

> The great and divine Apostle Paul with loud voice calls man created in the image of God, the body and temple of Christ. Excelling, therefore, every sensible creature, he who by the saving Passion has attained to the celestial dignity, eating and drinking Christ, is fitted in all respects for eternal life, sanctifying his soul and body by the participation of divine grace. Wherefore, if any one wishes to be a participator of the Immaculate Body in the time of the Synaxis, and to offer himself for the communion, let him draw near, arranging his hands in the form of a cross, and so let him receive the communion of grace. But such as, instead of their hands, make vessels of gold or other materials for the reception of the divine gift, and by these receive the immaculate communion, we by no means allow to come, as preferring inanimate and inferior matter to the image of God. But if any one shall be found imparting the immaculate Communion to those who bring vessels of this kind, let him be cut off as well as the one who brings them.[4]

Both of these were local councils which, by definition, would rarely determine the practice for the universal Church. Nonetheless, for the Western Church, Rouen obviously set the tone and direction of the eucharistic practice. Change would be inevitable. Communion in the hand had obviously evolved into a serious problem, and was slowly but surely destined to slip into the past. In due course, reverent Communion on the tongue would become the normal practice of eucharistic reception.

In the case of Trullo, the ruling emperor intended this synod to be an ecumenical council, but the pope refused to accept it as such. Still, the synod is recognized as authoritative by the East and is very influential on the code of canon law for the Eastern Catholic Churches today.

Then, as now, when it came to the manner of reception, disharmony reigned within the Church, and most certainly between the East and the West. Fortescue weighs in again, immediately following the time of St. Gregory I, demonstrating that change was difficult to accept: "For some time, both ways must have gone on side by side. Saint Bede (AD 735) mentions reception in the hand, the VIth Roman Ordo (IXth century) describes our way."[5]

What could have occurred prior to AD 650, possibly even back in the previous century, that necessitated such a striking change or regression in the Latin Church's manner of reception? Scholars have presented three theories; in all likelihood, each played a singularly unique role.

First, and seemingly most importantly, the challenge with Communion in the hand, then and now, is the ever-present danger of abuse. With Rouen, we have no written documentation noting the specific challenges facing the Church, but the strident language released by the synod speaks volumes. Whatever occurred, Rouen was pointedly explicit: Any priest or deacon placing the host in a lay person's hand would be barred from the altar "because he despises almighty God and dishonors what belongs to God."

In all likelihood, Communion in the hand enabled abuse from those who refused to recognize the Body of Christ, just as it does today. The resulting denial and confusion could also have logically played a part. The Synod of Rouen clearly recognized one of the Church's primary obligations: The Bread of Life must be protected at all costs, and it is the responsibility of the Church to lead the faithful in doing so. Anything else would dishonor God, and to dishonor God is to despise Him. The Church acted accordingly.

Second, sometime around the eighth century, the West began to use azyme (unleavened bread). It had always been assumed that Our Lord used azyme at the Last Supper. A conversion from leavened bread was met with little opposition in the West. (Again, a very different interpretation was held in the East.) The delicate pieces of thin wafer facilitated this method of distribution. Unlike the crumbled pieces of bread formerly used, the wafer easily adhered to the moist tongue. By the early second millennium, it became "normal and customary" to receive unleavened bread in the West.

The three giants of patrology—Jungmann, Fortescue, and Kucharek—all believed there was a connection between the use of unleavened bread and reception on the tongue, and that the adoption of unleavened bread may have contributed to the predominant shift in the manner of reception. Even considering the time span between Rouen and the eighth century, this is a reasonable assumption.

Third, Jungmann noted an ever-growing respect for the Eucharist which influenced the decision to switch to reverent Communion on the tongue. As we have seen, the Early Church recognized and encouraged adoration, veneration, and reverence in the presence of God, and the faithful responded accordingly.[6] Jungmann also wrote that, thanks to the distribution of Holy Communion directly into the mouth, several problems were solved: the necessity for those about to receive the Eucharist to clean their hands; the serious problem of preventing fragments of consecrated bread from being lost; and the necessity of purifying the patens of the hands after receiving the sacrament. The cloth and later on the paten were expressions of greater respect for the Eucharist.

At Rouen, a further rule was established that at High Mass the priest was to place the Eucharist into the hands of the deacon and subdeacon as *ministri altaris*. During the tenth and eleventh centuries, that right was narrowed down to priests and deacons.

Then it disappeared entirely, although there were still isolated accounts of the laity taking the Sacrament into their hands. In all likelihood, this would have been labeled an abuse.

While receiving reverently, standing appeared to be customary for most of the first millennium. Kneeling as a custom gradually gained ascendancy between the eleventh and sixteenth centuries. Jungmann noted many signs of adoration or reverence when communicating while standing, writing that "signs of veneration could naturally be taken for granted." He noted the following:

- St. Hildegard (d. AD 1179) had her nuns approach Communion dressed in white, adorned like brides, with a crown which displayed on the forehead the picture of the *Agnus Dei*.
- About the same time, when the Canons of the Lateran went to Communion, they all wore the cope.
- In Cluny, they were still speaking of the custom practiced by the Fathers of approaching *discalceatis pedibus* (barefoot).
- Reverence was also shown by bodily movement. The *Consuetudines* of Cluny, written down by Udalricus about AD 1080, demand a genuflection before receiving.
- Elsewhere it was customary to kiss the floor or the priest's foot.
- According to Theodore of Mopsuestia, the communicant should draw near with lowered eyes, both hands extended, and at the same time he should speak a word of adoration, since he is about to receive the Body of the King.
- There are a few sources which advise the communicant to remain in prayer momentarily before the reception; one should keep in mind the power of Him whose Body is held in one's hands, acknowledge one's own sinfulness and unworthiness, and praise the Lord *qui tale dedit tali.*[7]

Over the centuries, the Church has always characterized the moment of Holy Communion with sacredness and the greatest respect. To the best of her ability, the Church organically developed and embraced external signs in order to promote understanding of this great sacramental mystery. Moreover, the Church has continuously recognized its primary obligation to teach the faithful to receive Holy Communion with the right interior dispositions, among which stands out the need to comprehend and consider interiorly the Real Presence of Him Whom they are to receive. (See *The Catechism of Pope Pius X*, nos. 628, 636).[8]

In the Early Church, whether standing or kneeling, on the tongue or in the hand, receiving the Bread of Life, the greatest gift ever offered, required the utmost in reverence. To emphasize this, the sanctuary—the Holy of Holies, where God Himself resides—was distinctly separated from the remainder of the church. The manner of separation and the boundaries have changed throughout the centuries, but there is no doubt there was a clearly defined separation.

At the Council of Laodices in the fourth century, the laity received Holy Communion at the altar. In the seventh century, at the Fourth Council of Toledo, it was established that priests and deacons would receive in the sanctuary. From the thirteenth century, a white cloth was spread before the communicants kneeling before the altar, and in the sixteenth century, the cloth was spread on a bench set up outside the sanctuary. This eventually became the much-loved Communion rail.

By the thirteenth century, because of the danger of spilling the Blood of Christ, Communion under bread alone came to be preferred in some Western European countries. A couple hundred years later, singular reception became the norm in the Latin Church.[9] This was easily justified because one received the whole sacrament in one species.

Four hundred and fifty years ago, after sporadic meetings over eighteen years, the Council of Trent (1545–1563) closed its deliberations and forwarded its decisions to Rome for papal approval. Although plagued by intermittent attendance, sickness, military threats, and political machinations, in terms of Church doctrine the outcome of Trent was astonishing. No council has ever had a wider effect.

Trent, of course, was an exhaustive response to Protestant heresy, and transubstantiation and the Real Presence represented irrefutable Church dogma. Trent "openly and sincerely professes that after the consecration of the bread and wine, Our Lord Jesus Christ, true God and man, is really, truly and substantially contained in the Blessed Sacrament of the Holy Eucharist under the outward appearances of sensible things."

Our Savior is present in His humanity not only in His natural manner of existence at the right hand of the Father, but also at the same time in the sacrament of the Eucharist "in a manner of existing that we can hardly express in words but that our minds, illumined by faith, can come to see as possible to God and that we must most firmly believe."[10]

At Trent, the *Doctrine of Concomitance*—the belief of Our Lord's entire Presence in either element of the eucharistic Bread or Wine—was reaffirmed when the Church declared: "If anyone denies that Christ, the fountain and author of all graces, is received whole and entire under the one species of bread . . . let him be anathema."[11]

Thus, over 1,500 years all of this extraordinary adoration, veneration, and reverence grew organically within the Church, transforming the liturgy to glorify God and feed His people with the Sacred Species—without which there is no survival.

But first, prior to the Council of Trent, there was the Protestant Reformation—which began almost three decades earlier, in 1517—with its famous roster of reformers happily slashing and burning everything Catholic in name, belief, tradition, or practice. Their early primary targets: transubstantiation and the Real Presence.

A new eucharistic storm would soon engulf the Church, the first major tsunami propagated by the enemy within.

1 Fortescue, *The Mass*, 373.

2 Two different dates are routinely presented for the Synod of Rouen, and other Synods of Rouen are also possible. Whatever the actual date of this instruction might be, it doesn't change the dramatic impact that this synod had on the Latin Church.

3 H. T. Bruns, ed., *Canones Apostolorum et Conciliorum saeculorum*, vol. 2 (Charleston, SC: Nabu Press, 2011), 268–69.

4 Philip Schaff, ed., *A Select library of Nicene and post-Nicene Fathers of the Christian Church* (Grand Rapids, MI: Eerdmans Publishing Company, 1988), 407.

5 Fortescue, *The Mass*, 373.

6 Jungmann, *The Mass*, vol. 2, 381.

7 *Ibid.*, 374–78.

8 Office for the Liturgical Celebrations of the Supreme Pontiff, "Communion Received on the Tongue and While Kneeling," http://www.vatican.va/news_services/liturgy/details/ns_lit_doc_20091117_comunione_en.html.

9 This was greeted with dismay in the Eastern Church.

10 Council of Trent, Session XIII, *Decree Concerning the Most Holy Sacrament of the Eucharist*, ch. 1, http://www.ewtn.com/library/COUNCILS/TRENT13.HTM.

11 Council of Trent, Session XXI, Canon III, http://www.ewtn.com/library/COUNCILS/TRENT21.HTM.

CHAPTER SIX.

The Protestant Reformation

On March 21, 1556, at the pulpit on the day of his execution, Thomas Cranmer, the architect of the Edwardian Reformation, opened with a prayer and an exhortation to obey the king and queen. Then, unexpectedly, he ended his sermon by deviating from his prepared script. Cranmer renounced the recantations against Roman Catholicism that he had written or signed with his own hand. For this, he said, his hand would be punished by being burnt first. Cranmer then added, "And as for the pope, I refuse him, as Christ's enemy, and Antichrist with all his false doctrine."

Cranmer was pulled from the pulpit and taken to the stake. As the flames drew around him, he fulfilled his promise by placing his right hand into the heart of the fire while saying "that unworthy hand." His dying words were "Lord Jesus, receive my spirit. . . . I see the heavens open and Jesus standing at the right hand of God."[1]

Cranmer's words and actions galvanized the Edwardian (English) Reformation like nothing else ever could.

The beliefs and methodology envisioned and implemented by Cranmer have altered the spiritual landscape of Britain, its Anglican colonies, and the entire world for close to half a millennium. The path he avowed continues to reverberate within the Anglican Church and across mainline Protestantism, right up until today.

In 1529, a meeting between Cranmer and two of his Cambridge associates—both advisors to King Henry VIII—dramatically altered the lives of Cranmer and his king. The British monarch had a fierce desire to secure a divorce. Cranmer offered a unique solution: set aside the legal case for annulment in Rome in favor of canvassing theologians from European universities. Their opinions, he counseled, could have merit, even in Rome.

The idea was presented to King Henry, who welcomed it. Cranmer was soon invited to join a royal team that was chartered to implement his solution and garner responses.

In time, two documents were produced: the *Collectanea Satis Copiosa* ("The Sufficiently Abundant Collections") and *The Determinations*, both historical and theological support for the argument that the king exercised supreme jurisdiction within his realm. Cranmer argued the case as part of the embassy to Rome in 1530, and in 1532 was appointed ambassador to Holy Roman Emperor Charles V.

On March 30, 1533, Cranmer was named Archbishop of Canterbury. Once his appointment was approved by the pope, Cranmer declared King Henry's marriage to Catherine null and void. Four months later, the king married Anne Boleyn. In 1536, she was executed, and the king married Jane Seymour. When Seymour died, the king took Anne of Cleves to be his wife in 1540. In the same year he divorced her and married Catherine Howard, who would be executed in 1542. His sixth and last wife—Catherine Parr—survived him.

From his secure position as a royal advisor, the archbishop defended an implicit belief in the divine right of kings. In his mind, there were no limits on the ecclesiastical authority of kings; they were as fully the representatives of the Church as the state, and Cranmer hardly distinguished between the two.

As the king divorced or executed his many wives one by one, Cranmer continued to bask in King Henry's favor. The two men remained close for the rest of the king's life. Cranmer was at his side when Henry died in 1547.

The highly public divorces of King Henry VIII severed the English Church from the Holy See of Rome. The right to divorce, however, was just one of many disagreements Cranmer had with the Roman Catholic

Church. As early as 1538, Cranmer repudiated the Catholic dogma of transubstantiation—the changing of the elements of the bread and wine, when they are consecrated in the Eucharist, into the Body and Blood of Christ. Cranmer was simply reflecting Continental reformers with similar beliefs.

Thus, a powerful new eucharistic storm was unleashed throughout Europe, a dramatic force that emanated from enemies operating deep within the Roman Catholic Church. Their primary target: the Catholic dogma of transubstantiation and the Real Presence.

In 1549, when he completed *The Book of Common Prayer*, Cranmer included his views on this core Catholic belief:

> Transubstantiation, of the change of the substance of Bread and Wine in the Supper of the Lord, cannot be proved by Holy Writ; but is repugnant to the plain words of Scripture, overthroweth the nature of a Sacrament, and hath given occasion to many superstitions.[2]

Thomas Cranmer became the first archbishop of the new Church of England. One of his early objectives for the newly minted Church was to create a more biblical mode of worship, cleansed from foreign "Romish superstitions." Paradoxically, he strived to preserve as much Catholic liturgy as possible, in large measure because change was unwelcome in many quarters.

Still, maintaining any semblance of traditional Catholic liturgy failed to satisfy many of Cranmer's fellow reformers; nor did they truly appreciate Cranmer's 1549 edition of *The Book of Common Prayer.* A second Edwardian Prayer Book was planned, this one designed to sever any lingering liturgical cords with Rome. For guidance on the new project, Cranmer turned to a handful of Continental reformers, many of whom were residing in England.

Among their number was Martin Bucer, an early pioneer of ecumenism, who had personal experience with the challenge facing Cranmer: a need to impose reform on a reluctant clergy, and the consequent requirement to proceed cautiously. Bucer had already been expelled from Strasbourg for his reformation activities. He also was deeply involved in the failed reform of the archdiocese of Cologne. Based on his experience, Bucer was sympathetic to pacing liturgical reform, as well as to preserving a larger measure of outward continuity in liturgical matters.

Bucer's evaluation of *The Book of Common Prayer* resulted in a document of written advice subsequently known as the *Censura*. In it, Bucer endorsed short-term continuity in order to ensure far-reaching future reform. A substantial part of the *Censura* addressed what Bucer believed to be weaknesses of the 1549 book; in particular, he was concerned with a perceived threat from Catholic clerical traditionalists.

More importantly, Bucer addressed the rubrics relating to the administration of Communion. He was determined to revise the conduct of the service, and specifically targeted any "superstitious" practice, which he addressed in the conclusion of the *Censura*:

> There are people who endeavour to represent that Mass of theirs . . . with all the outward show they can, with vestments and lights, with bowings and crossings, with washing the chalice and other gestures from the Missal, with breathing over the bread and the chalice of the eucharist, with moving the book on the table from the right side of it to the left, with setting the table in the same place where the altar used to stand, with displaying the bread and the chalice of the eucharist to poor little old men [and women?] and to others filled with superstition, who adore them and yet do not communicate in the sacraments.[3]

Another of Bucer's principal concerns was that "rigid uniformity" might foster a "superstitious" reverence for the bread, and for this reason it would be suitable to use ordinary bread. The statement at the end of this rubric (explaining that no one must think to receive less of Christ in a part of the bread than in the whole) should be extended to ensure that the Body of Christ is not to be thought of as "locally shut up inside" each piece.

The rubric directing the bread to be placed in the mouth of the communicant would now require the bread to be placed into the communicant's hands. This was in keeping with the practice among the Strasbourg churches, where the broken bread was distributed into the hands of communicants and the chalice passed from hand to hand.

The *Censura* further directed that, in preparation for the sacrament, the priest take only as much bread and wine as needed to serve the communicants who were present. Otherwise, it might give rise to "superstition" regarding the consecrated elements, leading the laity to believe that the elements were different after consecration. Bucer stressed that it was necessary to make people understand that, apart from their use at the communion service itself, the elements remain bread and wine.

When *The Book of Common Prayer*'s 1552 edition was published, it included Cranmer's rejection of the Real Presence. In Article XXIX, "Of the Wicked which do not eat the Body of Christ in the use of the Lord's Supper," he wrote:

> The Wicked, and such as be void of a lively faith, although they do carnally and visibly press with their teeth, as Saint Augustine saith, the Sacrament of the Body and Blood of Christ, yet in no wise are they partakers of Christ: but rather to their condemnation, do eat and drink the sign, or Sacrament, of so great a thing.[4]

Cranmer, of course, was simply responding to Martin Bucer, who demanded that Communion be given in the hand to bring it into line with the Continental Protestant practice. In *Censura,* the reasons Bucer presented for insisting on this change were explicit:

> In fact, I have no doubt that this usage of not putting these sacraments in the hands of the faithful has been introduced out of a

> double superstition; firstly, the false honour they wished to show to this sacrament, and secondly the wicked arrogance of priests claiming greater holiness than that of the people of Christ, by virtue of the oil of consecration. The Lord undoubtedly gave these, His sacred symbols, into the hands of the Apostles, and no one who has read the records of the ancients can be in doubt that this was the usage observed in the churches until the advent of the Roman Antichrist.
>
> As, therefore, every superstition of the Roman Anti-Christ is to be detested, and the simplicity of Christ, and the Apostles, and the ancient Churches, is to be recalled, I should wish that pastors and teachers of the people should be commanded that each is faithfully to teach the people that it is superstitious and wicked to think that the hands of those who truly believe in Christ are less pure than their mouths; or that the hands of the ministers are holier than the hands of the laity; so that it would be wicked, or less fitting, as was formerly wrongly believed by the ordinary folk, for the laity to receive these sacraments in the hand: and therefore that the indications of this wicked belief be removed. . . .
>
> In that way good men will be easily brought to the point of all receiving the sacred symbols in the hand, conformity in receiving will be kept, and there will be safeguards against all furtive abuse of the sacraments. *For, although for a time concession can be made to those whose faith is weak, by giving them the Sacraments in the mouth when they so desire, if they are carefully taught they will soon conform themselves to the rest of the Church and take the Sacraments in the hand.* (emphasis added)[5]

The eucharistic storm surged, the reformers "inventing" as they plunged forward: an evolving, man-centered liturgy featuring an entirely new "Communion Service" denying transubstantiation. They ignored or disdained the knowledge of tradition and theology spanning fifteen hundred years of Christianity. They pretended that the Early Church Fathers and teachers, every great scholar, writer and theologian, all the saints, and every faithful Christian, the vast majority of whom had revered and adored the Real Presence, were all wrong.

Remarkably enough, no record exists of a single Early Church Father or teacher ever denying the Real Presence. In *The Emergence of the Catholic Tradition: 100 – 600,* the first volume of Jaroslav Pelikan's classic series *The Christian Tradition: A History of the Development of Doctrine,* Pelikan (a non-Catholic) observed that "no orthodox father of the second or third century of whom we have record... declared the presence of the body and blood of Christ in the Eucharist to be no more than symbolic..."[6]

None of that mattered, nor made a shred of difference, to English and Continental reformers.

This, then, is the essence of Communion in the hand of the sixteenth century: a recognizably anti-Catholic practice, rooted in utter disbelief in the Real Presence and the priesthood, completely disconnected from the Church's traditional past, resulting in a total rejection of Catholicism. Communion in the hand was, in fact, a highly visible and purposeful denial of transubstantiation and the Real Presence.

Why, then, just a few hundred years later, did so many millions of Catholics elect to follow sixteenth-century reformers to the letter, and still do so today?

Through the imperfect lens of history, almost half a millennium later, there are lessons to be learned. Once one denies transubstantiation and the Real Presence, one is quite willing to question and reject any other dogmatic belief, or any traditional Catholic practice or tradition. Within just a few years after the Edwardian Reformation, altars became wooden communion "tables," prayers for the dead were deleted, and vestments were banned. The confessional-style forgiving of sins was discontinued, and in its place was the remission of sins through preaching the Gospel.

The entire Communion Service was substantially modified. The Holy Eucharist became broken bread, received in the hand while standing in order to eradicate any belief in the physical presence of God Himself; and the sacred vessels, no longer sacrosanct, were passed from hand to hand. Adoration was obliterated as if it had never existed. Images of the saints, and most notably images of the Blessed Virgin Mary, revered since the time of Christ, were banned from countess churches around the globe. The reverence, beauty, and art of 1,500 years of Catholicism were all abolished. "Romish superstitions" were wiped out in a single generation in favor of a man-made religion.

It would be pointless to argue that Thomas Cranmer was anything but sincere in his beliefs. Nonetheless, 35,000 man-made Protestant sects, virtually all of them, one way or another, following Cranmer's erroneous lead, each one with a different and widely conflicting belief system, are living proof that Cranmer was wrong. Almost five hundred years after his death, history speaks for itself.

One could expect that Catholic progressives of the twentieth and twenty-first centuries, presumably well-educated and versed in Church history and theology, *must* have known of the bitter fruits harvested from the Reformation. They also had to be well aware that half a century of failure to teach or even mention transubstantiation and the Real Presence—together with the deliberate minimization and marginalization of traditional beliefs and practices—could lead to a eucharistic storm unlike anything ever experienced in the 2,000-year history of Catholicism.

Yet in the aftermath of Vatican II, virtually all the failed innovations and banal novelties of the Edwardian Reformation—including Communion in the hand while standing—have been mirrored in the Church, one way or the other, worldwide.

The almost universal acceptance of innovations and abuses is an open portal to unending chaos. One glance at a multitude of man-made religions will confirm this truism: Not surprisingly, in order to move with the times, cultural "advances" continue to emerge and are routinely adopted. Contraception, abortion, same-sex marriage, women priests and bishops, in vitro fertilization, and euthanasia arrived one after another.

Needless to say, many, and sometimes all, of these "modern" advances have been routinely adopted and sponsored by Catholic progressives inside the Church, openly or surreptitiously. We can be confident that any advance, innovation, or novelty yet unrealized will undoubtedly make an appearance, in one Catholic church or another, sooner or later. The only requirement is time.

Pope Benedict XVI summed it up well: "The greatest persecution of the Church comes not from her enemies without, but arises from sin within the Church."[7]

The enemy isn't at the gate; the enemy is deep within the walls.

1 Claire Ridgeway, "The Execution of Thomas Cranmer," http://www.theanneboleynfiles.com/the-execution-of-thomas-cranmer.

2 *The Book of Common Prayer and the Holy Bible* (New York: Church Publishing, 2007), 873.

3 Note Bucer's small "e," not uncommon for the times; N. Scott Amos, "Martin Bucer and the Revision of the 1549 Book of Common Prayer: Reform of Ceremonies and the Didactic Use of Ritual," *Reformation & Renaissance Review* 2 (1999): 118, http://www.martinsvianna.net/artigos/it3/BUCER_AND_ENGLISH_BOOK_OF_PRAYER.pdf.

4 See Article XXIX, "The Articles of Religion, Book of Common Prayer," http://justus.anglican.org/resources/bcp/1928/Articles.htm.

5 E. C. Whitaker, ed., *Martin Bucer and the Book of Common Prayer* (Great Wakering, UK: Mayhew-McCrimmon, 1974).

6 Jeroslav Pelikan, *Emergence Of The Catholic Tradition: 100-600, Volume One – The Christian Tradition: A History of the Development of Doctrine* (University of Chicago, 1975): 167

7 Peter Seewald, *Light of the World: The Pope, the Church, and the Signs of the Times* (San Francisco: Ignatius Press, 2010), 27.

CHAPTER SEVEN

The Wake of Modernism

The December 17, 1965 over-sized cover of *Life Magazine* featured the last session of the epic venture of Vatican II. A spectacular scene was captured from the dome of St. Peter's: Looking down in the circular distance one could make out a blur of 2,300 tiny prelates, gathered together in a sea of red, sitting on bleachers in the basilica, side by side.

After four long, grueling years, the Council was over.

The prelates would return to a Church embroiled in "renewal" and transformation. *Life* intoned that the new Church would be "less preoccupied with the City of God and more in love with the City of Man. Such was the general purport of what this great council did to the spirit and structure of the Church." And later, "It (Vatican II) has brought the 400-year Reformation era of Western history to an end and opened a new one that will end no man knows where."

Almost half a century later, we assuredly know one thing for sure: Something went terribly wrong after Vatican II.

Certainly, many attribute the outward mass migration of Catholics—a catastrophic toll that easily numbers well more than 100 million souls—to a handful of vague, confusing documents released from the Second Vatican Council, complete with what Michael Davies famously referred to as "time bombs."

However, the preponderance of historical evidence demonstrates that it was neo-modernists who took advantage of the Council's documents—and a few that followed—interpreting, revising, or ignoring them any way they wanted, apparently with encouragement at the highest levels of the Church.

More than half a century earlier, in 1907, Pope Saint Pius X – revered as one of the Church's greatest popes – declared war on the heresy of modernism.

The Church first took note of the heresy of modernism and defined it on September 26, 1835. It condemned the approach of certain priests and professors in German universities, who were using the modern philosophy of Descartes, Kant, and Hegel to reinterpret the Articles of Faith. It was said that "they are profaning their teaching office and are adulterating the sacred Deposit of Faith."[1]

From the very onset of its introduction to the faith, modernism was condemned by the Church in the Holy Office's decree of *Lamentabili Sane*, plus various other pronouncements to follow. Nevertheless, modernism continued to flourish, largely due to its vague and ambiguous nature.

Pius X viewed modernism as a massive threat to the Church, referring to it as the "synthesis of all heresies." In that same year of 1907, on the feast of Our Lady's Nativity, his renowned encyclical *Pascendi Dominici Gregis* was promulgated. In it, Pius X wrote something that, from the perspective of more than a century later, is both prescient and frightening:

> Though they express astonishment themselves, no one can justly be surprised that We number such men among the enemies of the Church . . . the most pernicious of all the adversaries of the Church. For as We have said, they put their designs for her ruin into operation not from without but from within; hence, the danger is present almost in the very veins and heart of the Church, whose injury is the more certain, the more intimate is their knowledge of her. Moreover they lay the axe not to the branches and shoots, but to the very root, that is, to the faith and its deepest fires. *And having struck at this root of immortality, they proceed to disseminate*

poison through the whole tree, so that there is no part of Catholic truth from which they hold their hand, none that they do not strive to corrupt.[2] (emphasis added)

Three years later, in 1910, Pope Saint Pius X issued the *Oath of Modernism*, required by all clergy, pastors, confessors, preachers, religious superiors, and professors in philosophical-theological seminaries. The oath stated, in part:

- I profess that God, the origin and end of all things, can be known with certainty by the natural light of reason from the created world;
- [I] sincerely hold that the doctrine of faith was handed down to us from the apostles through the orthodox Fathers in exactly the same meaning and always in the same purport;
- [I] reject that method of judging and interpreting Sacred Scripture which [departs] from the tradition of the Church, the analogy of faith, and the norms of the Apostolic See;
- [I] declare that I am completely opposed to the error of the modernists who hold that there is nothing divine in sacred tradition;
- [I] firmly hold, then, and shall hold to my dying breath the belief of the Fathers in the charism of truth, which certainly is, was, and always will be in the succession of the episcopacy from the apostles. The purpose of this is, then, not that dogma may be tailored according to what seems better and more suited to the culture of each age; rather, that the absolute and immutable truth preached by the apostles from the beginning may never be believed to be different, may never be understood in any other way;
- [I] promise that I shall keep all these articles faithfully, entirely, and sincerely, and guard them inviolate, in no way deviating from them in teaching or in any way in word or in writing;
- Thus I promise, this I swear, so help me God.

The oath was required until July 1967, when the Congregation for the Doctrine of the Faith rescinded it. How could it not? By then progressives had interpreted, revised, and applied the documents of Vatican II in any way they wanted, with little or no opposition. The oath was counter-productive and quickly disappeared.

What specifically is the heresy of modernism?

Modernism is a movement that grew out of Enlightenment rationalism in the late eighteenth and early nineteenth centuries. The inevitable fruit of Protestant "private judgment" eventually began to lead minds to reject the veracity of Sacred Scripture. Modernists have more faith in "science" than they do in divine revelation, be it from Scripture or Tradition; when they try to reconcile the two, science supersedes faith.

Christian belief is routinely sacrificed to satisfy scientific advancements. Modernist exegetes are more than willing to accept the absurd claims of rationalist philosophers like Kant and Hegel: They reject that there is a divine truth, or any "truth," to be known, and that all we call "truth" are simply the vagaries of the human mind.[3]

Modernist progressives insist that the Church move with the times and update its core beliefs. For almost 2,000 years, the One, Holy, Catholic, and Apostolic Church has been the harbor of eternal, objective truth, revealed by Almighty God Himself. Rather than accept these truths from a timeless God, modernists demand that the Church constantly update truth to reflect the current culture, however changing or temporary it might be.

As faithful Catholics, we must believe in the objective reality of the supernatural. There is a heaven and a hell, and the Annunciation really happened. The Virgin Mary is the Mother of Jesus, and salvation is possible through forgiveness from our Savior. The Resurrection opened the doors to paradise. The Real Presence is the Body, Blood, Soul, and Divinity of Our Lord Jesus Christ in the Holy Eucharist.

These Roman Catholic truths are irrefutable and non-negotiable.

Unless, of course, you're a neo-modernist, in which case you might comfortably reject anything you "feel" comfortable with.

Neo-modernists believe that faith in doctrine is derived from a certain interior sense all humans have, and from this sense comes a need of the divine manifested in religious sentiment. In various ways, neo-modernists believe that Catholicism should be based not, as hitherto, on reason, but rather on *experience*.

The exaltation of experience above reason is the essence of the modernist heresy.

Neo-modernists incorrectly believe that one religion is just as good as another, and none are any more sacred than the other. They believe all religions derived from man can be manipulated by man to fit any situation. God, eternity, and truth have absolutely nothing to do with it. The ideal, in fact, could be a one-world church in which no one is separated by so-called truth or dogma.

In his pontificate, Pope Saint Pius X fought back valiantly, by word and deed, affirming with crystal clarity that the Catholic faith is founded on reason, and that the Church's dogmas do not depend on religious experience, but were revealed by God to the Apostles and cannot change. For the pope, the proximate cause of modernism "consists in a perversion of the mind" and ignorance:

> The intellectual cause of Modernism, . . . and the chief one, is ignorance. Yes, these very Modernists who seek to be esteemed as Doctors of the Church, who speak so loftily of modern philosophy and show such contempt for scholasticism, have embraced the one with all of its false glamour, precisely because their ignorance of the other has left them without the means of being able to recognize confusion of thought and to refute sophistry. Their whole system, containing as it does errors so many and so great, has been born of the union between faith and false philosophy.[4]

Ultimately, His Holiness prevailed. Among his many other feats, he protected the Real Presence from the whims of neo-modernists, thereby defeating a virulent eucharistic storm. Modernism receded into darkness, but continued to simmer on, especially in Europe. For the next half century, it operated quietly, seemingly dormant, but never far away.

The unintended catalyst in resurrecting the synthesis of all heresies was Vatican II. Modernism's loyal adherents were emboldened by the vaguely worded documents released by the Council in 1965. Neo-modernists—hiding in plain sight—interpreted and revised the new documents from Rome to reflect their own convoluted agendas. An unknown but significant number of cardinals, bishops, priests, deacons, nuns, and faithful slowly commenced a fifty-year journey of rejecting one core Catholic belief or practice after another, each one according to his own experience, how he felt at a particular time, or perhaps even how that belief affected his lifestyle.

The dominating influence of modernism explains widespread "cafeteria Catholicism," in which one picks and chooses whatever "feels" right, convenient, or comfortable at a given moment in time. As a consequence, Catholicism is often no longer a set tradition of worship in which the Faith is practiced and lived, but a series of ever-changing beliefs cooked into one unholy soup—a synthesis of heresies. In effect, a Catholic neo-modernist creates his own universe, any way he wants it, however he wants it, no matter the cost. *I believe it, and therefore it is true.* Here, within this false philosophy, we can readily see the errors and destruction that freely and openly emanate, with little or no opposition, from within and without the walls of the Church.

At one time or another, most of us have attended one Catholic Mass or another that seemed more Protestant than Catholic. Yet we wonder why our children are confused, doubtful, indifferent, and deserting *en masse*. To a significant degree, the answer is modernism with its utter and on-going wake of destruction.

In 1964, Pope Paul VI appointed a committee—*Consilium ad exsequendam Constitutionem de Sacra Liturgia*—to direct the on-going liturgical renewal. The Vincentian priest Annibale Bugnini, considered to be one of the primary architects of Vatican II, was its secretary. In

1965, Fr. Bugnini stated in *L'Osservatore Romano* that the Consilium's task was to remove from the Roman Liturgy "everything that could constitute the slightest risk of a stumbling block or a source of displeasure for our Separated Brethren, that is, for the Protestants."[5]

In order to achieve a one-world church, the Real Presence has *always* been the ultimate target of serious progressives, and always will be. The Real Presence in the Blessed Sacrament—God Himself, the heart and soul of Roman Catholicism—is an ecumenical stumbling block that must be deprecated and abandoned, just as it was during the Reformation—or, at the very least, marginalized and trivialized, as it often is today. Otherwise, the great modernist experiment could ultimately fail.

Back in the early twentieth century, what particularly disturbed Pius X was that modernists continued to use Catholic formulas of faith for their own purposes, even when they ceased to believe in them. Modernists might consider truth and dogma to be irrelevant, but at the very least they could represent useful symbols. Thus, progressives, from the Reformation right up until today, have denied or downplayed the dogma of the Real Presence but rallied around its symbolism: We are, they rationalized, "fed" by the Word of God. Thus, the *meal* or *banquet* was in, and the *Real Presence* was out.

Standing to receive in the hand would be perfectly fine and would also go a long way to show that bread is bread.

There is no doubt of the destructive wake achieved by neo-modernists. Going forward, we should be cognizant that their work continues without respite. Still, there are fresh, faithful breezes emanating from the Vatican. Forty-three years after its introduction, Rome is trying to restore reverence to the Novus Ordo liturgy, where it is being welcomed and well received.

Meanwhile, the Traditional Latin Mass, hated with a passion by every doting progressive, was considered to be all but dead and buried. With the release of Paul VI's Novus Ordo Mass in 1969, progressives almost succeeded in burying the Mass of the Ages, but ostracized traditionalists refused to surrender. In fact, they fought back valiantly against a determined hierarchy that blocked them at every step. In 1988, Pope John Paul II—responding to increasingly vociferous traditionalists—issued a *motu proprio Ecclesia Dei*, urging wide acceptance of the Tridentine Mass. It was opposed worldwide. Pope Benedict XVI achieved much greater success with his 2007 *Summorum Pontificum*, authorizing parish priests to celebrate the Tridentine Rite with or without their bishop's permission.

To the utter dismay of neo-modernists everywhere, the Traditional Latin Mass is back and growing worldwide.

For the first time in almost half a century, a Pontifical High Mass was offered in St. Peter's Basilica in Rome. Archbishop Raymond Burke (now Cardinal Burke) celebrated the Mass of the Ages on October 18, 2009. Three years later, in November 2012, the Traditional Latin Mass was celebrated on the main altar at St. Peter's. The Pontifical High Mass celebrant was the prefect of the Congregation for Divine Worship, Cardinal Cañizares Llovera. It was the first time since the publication of the papal permission *Summorum Pontificum* in July of 2007 that a Prefect of the Congregation for Divine Worship celebrated Mass in the Old Rite.

At the heart of that scorned liturgy is the beloved Real Presence, adored with a deep fervor that spans the generations over two millennia. The Traditional Latin Mass continues its re-emergence around the globe, parish by parish, nation after nation—very slowly, but very surely. Just as portentous, traditional seminaries are packed wall to wall.

This is not at all what neo-modernists imagined for the twenty-first century—not even close. They are deeply alarmed, and have no intention of surrendering without a fight. After all, if modernism teaches us anything, it is this: Modernists are right because, in their universe, they just are. Whatever they believe, whatever they think or experience, is valid. Dogma and objective truth are nothing more than words, and words simply don't count; at a minimum, they can be ignored, disdained, and even scorned, as they often are. The Real Presence in the Blessed Sacrament deserves nothing more than a slight nod of the head.

In the midst of a momentous eucharistic storm that is terrifyingly quiet, that is often all He can expect.

1 Raymond Taouk, "Modernism—A Catholic Refutation," http://www.catholicapologetics.info/modernproblems/modernism/modnsm.htm.
2 Pope St. Pius X, *Pascendi Dominici Gregis*, 3, http://www.vatican.va/holy_father/pius_x/encyclicals/documents/hf_p-x_enc_19070908_pascendi-dominici-gregis_en.html.
3 Larry Roach, "What Modernists (and Neo-modernists) Believe—Pt. 1," http://veneremurcernui.wordpress.com/2013/10/09/what-modernists-and-neo-modernists-believe-pt-1.
4 Pope St. Pius X, *Pascendi*, 41, http://www.vatican.va/holy_father/pius_x/encyclicals/documents/hf_p-x_enc_19070908_pascendi-dominici-gregis_en.html.
5 *L'Osservatore Romano*, March 19, 1965.

CHAPTER EIGHT

Storm Watch

Three years after the closing chapter of Vatican II, an ordinary event occurred in American Catholicism that would be, over time, transformational by any standard. The potentiality of what transpired would not—in fact, could not—be perceived, nor even imagined, in the slightest. The event was destined to turn the powerful Roman Catholic Church, gradually and imperceptibly at first, in subtle ways not easy definable—not just in America, but in Rome and around the world. At the time, no one had any idea—not even Archbishop John Dearden of Detroit.[1]

Famously progressive, deeply involved in the work of the Second Vatican Council, "Iron John" Dearden helped shape a handful of the Council's doctrinal documents. After Vatican II, he drew national attention with his innovative approach to the new liturgy. In the mid-1970's, Dearden headed a Church committee that undertook a two-year study of public issues. Hearings and debates involved 1,350 delegates from 150 dioceses, all of whom were selected by their bishops. Remarkably, the committee adopted a five-year, 182-point "Call to Action" agenda at a 1976 conference in Detroit, and submitted it to the Conference of Bishops. Included on the list were questionable, perhaps even heretical, proposals that went against such basic Church tenets as divorce, contraception, and the ordination of women.

Although Dearden took no exception to any of the proposals, the Conference of Bishops did; every proposal was shelved by time, always the most potent decision maker, and allowed mercifully to die.

A decade earlier, in 1966, Abp. John Dearden was elected president of the U.S. National Conference of Catholic Bishops (NCCB). At the time, the Conference was nowhere near the powerhouse it was destined to become, yet Dearden must surely have recognized the possibilities. He identified the need for a capable manager, someone, most critically, who shared his deeply ingrained progressive convictions. The position required a well-versed Vatican II neo-modernist, one who was highly intelligent and ambitious—a tenacious individual, someone with charisma and personality who could sway individuals and groups with equanimity.

In 1968, Dearden invited his protégé, Joseph Bernardin, then the Auxiliary Bishop of Atlanta, to become the first general secretary of the NCCB. This was the transformational event that no one could possibly have imagined, a quiet, unheralded appointment that was, in effect, the harbinger of a major eucharistic storm. It was imperceptible, but certain. There was a critical role to play, and Joseph Bernardin would play it well.

No one would ever question Bernardin's consummate proficiency. In 1966, when he was appointed a bishop, Bernardin was just thirty-eight years old, then the youngest prelate in the United States. As first general secretary of the NCCB at only forty years of age, he was on a fast track to prominence. Later, as archbishop of Cincinnati and then cardinal-archbishop of Chicago, Bernardin's leadership style evolved so skillfully, and his charismatic persona engaged so effectively, that he became the de facto face of American Catholicism.

His term as first general secretary would last four years, but Bernardin returned as president of the NCCB in 1974. A striking increase in power, potentiality, and influence materialized with the new role. Under his leadership, what was meant to be a do-little bishops' trade association was soon converted into a liberal-progressive think tank.[2] His style was to serve as a calm innovator in pursuit of a liberal agenda, all the while keeping a nervous Rome at bay.

Eugene Kennedy, Bernardin's long-time friend and biographer, describes these years well. He wrote about the Cincinnati archbishop working with the apostolic delegate to the United States, Abp. Jean Jadot. One mutual objective was to name "younger, conciliar-minded bishops in top dioceses throughout the country." These were men who "might have been personally sympathetic to even more radical transformations" but who, with Bernardin's guidance, refrained from challenging "positions which the aging Pope, Paul VI, had defended many times."

These Catholics, many priests and religious men and women among them, "were anxious, among other issues, to explore the possibilities of modifying the priestly obligation of celibacy and of ordaining women."[3]

Bernardin's modus operandi functioned so admirably that his influence on the Conference, and axiomatically on all of Catholicism, is still palpable today. Under his watch, the term "Bernardin's machine" came into vogue. As George Weigel wrote in *First Things*, it was symbolic of a force to be reckoned with:

> For the machine was quite rigorous in enforcing its ecclesiology and its politics, and it was perfectly capable of withdrawing its favor when bishops once thought loyal club members showed signs of intellectual or ecclesiastical independence.[4]

During this seminal period after Vatican II, Joseph Bernardin became the undisputed dominant figure among his brothers in the U.S. hierarchy. As such, he directed a potent network of prelates that dominated the affairs of U.S. Catholicism for over a quarter of a century. The clerics who most strongly supported him became known as "Bernardin's boys," and they were amply rewarded. Again, from George Weigel:

> He was succeeded as conference president by five men (John Quinn, John Roach, James Malone, John May, and Daniel Pilarczyk) who were all members of the Bernardin machine, and whose positions in the U.S. Church had no little to do with Bernardin's service on the Vatican's Congregation for Bishops (which Andrew Greeley once dubbed the "patronage office") and Bernardin's relationship

> with Belgian archbishop Jean Jadot, the Vatican representative in Washington from 1974 to 1980. In those halcyon days, Bernardin, master of the scene, could, with quiet confidence and no fear of contradiction, tell fellow American clerics that, "No, Jim Malone won't be the next archbishop of Cincinnati, but he will be the next president of the conference."[5]

From this seat of unprecedented power and influence, Bernardin ruled. Two specific initiatives he deployed still thrive today, both of which greatly impacted the Church.

Certainly his most famous initiative was "social justice," emulated by neo-modernists around the globe. Under Bernardin's expert guidance, social justice issues jumped on the bus of Catholicism and quickly moved to the front seats: War and peace, opposition to the death penalty, welfare reform, unemployment, and civil liberties would all take on a leading new emphasis in the Church.[6] By default—without a word of disfavor—sin, confession, purgatory, heaven, tradition, final judgment, and hell were relegated to the back seats, where they often would rarely ever see the light of day.

Catholic progressives loved it, and so did non-Catholics. In 1982, Bernardin's peace activism landed him on the cover of *Time Magazine*.

By then the cardinal-archbishop of Chicago, Bernardin asserted that the social teaching of the Church was a "seamless garment" in which abortion was treated as one concern among many. In 1983, he delivered these remarks in the Gannon Lecture at Fordham University:

> Those who defend the right to life of the weakest among us must be equally visible in support of the quality of life of the powerless among us: the old and the young, the hungry and the homeless, the undocumented immigrant and the unemployed worker.
>
> Consistency means that we cannot have it both ways. We cannot urge a compassionate society and vigorous public policy to protect

> the rights of the unborn and then argue that compassion and significant public programs on behalf of the needy undermine the moral fiber of the society or are beyond the proper scope of governmental responsibility.[7]

This statement, which came to be taken as authoritative throughout the American Church and beyond, proved, as Joseph Sobran observed, "to be nothing but a loophole for hypocritical Catholic politicians. If anything," he added, "it has actually made it easier for them than for non-Catholics to give their effective support to legalized abortion—that is, it has allowed them to be inconsistent and unprincipled about the very issues that Cardinal Bernardin said demand consistency and principle."[8]

The damage has been incalculable. A shocking number of American Catholic politicians suddenly felt comfortable endorsing a pro-abortion platform, and continue to do so. Simultaneously, the Church clergy all but abandoned the case against *Roe v. Wade.* Pro-lifers were essentially thrown under the bus, an unfortunate side effect of the "seamless garment" initiative.

The new social justice mantra developed a life of its own. Like a contagious virus, it raced around the world, often to be accepted at face value by millions of Catholic faithful. Yet unlike any other virus, the season never ended. Instead, Bernardin's innovative mantra still occupies the front seats in a multitude of dioceses and parishes worldwide. Only in the last decade or so has the Church's traditions—together with sin, confession, purgatory, heaven, final judgment, and hell—made somewhat of a comeback, moving up once again front and center to many, but far from all, Catholic parishes.

Bernardin's other lasting initiative preceded social justice, yet the two were inextricably connected. Social justice was a misleading derivative of "conciliar reform" that slowly but surely pushed traditional Catholic practices and beliefs deep into the background. One of those practices was Communion on the tongue. Eugene Kennedy provides us with a revealing window into a mindset and a time not too long past:

> So, for example, there were lengthy discussions about the new liturgical provision that allowed Catholics, as a symbol of their adult status, to receive the Eucharistic wafer in their hands. . . . To some conservative Catholics, communion in the hand was a desacralizing sign of the generalized failure of discipline that had crept into Church life. To Catholics encouraged by conciliar reform to practice their faith by attempting to influence the major issues of the time—war, racial relations, poverty and hunger—such an obsession with a minor issue was emblematic of an older, closed, and self-complacent Catholicism.[9]

Thus, the progressive mentality of the 70s and 80s, right up until today, is clearly illuminated. In the eyes of progressives, traditional Catholics were, and still are, little more than neo-Luddites, living in the past and blocking a promising new future, free from antiquated doctrine to focus on what is really important: social justice as defined by neo-modernists, replete with ever-changing values and ideologies. The obvious place for traditionalists was right beside pro-lifers: under the bus, which was where they promptly found themselves. (Often, of course, they were one and the same.)

The "minor issue" of Communion in the hand had emerged as another progressive mantra, championed by Bernardin and cherished by every authentic neo-modernist. Birthed in European disobedience, nourished by rogue prelates, Communion in the hand was reluctantly permitted as an exception to the rule by Paul VI, but the rule swallowed the exception and the practice disseminated to the four corners of the earth. It was, as history demonstrates, eagerly adopted by progressives everywhere. Similar to the social justice mantra, Communion in the hand negatively affected the Church and its faithful people, and continues to do so today.

The indult of *Memoriale Domini*, allowing Communion in the hand under very specific rules, was promulgated by Pope Paul VI on May 29, 1969. One of his directives pointedly declared that "contrary usage" was the prevailing practice for any nation seeking permission to practice Communion in the hand:

> *Where a contrary usage, that of placing holy communion on the hand, prevails,* the Holy See—wishing to help them fulfill their task, often difficult as it is nowadays—lays on those conferences the task of weighing carefully whatever special circumstances may exist there, taking care to avoid any risk of lack of respect or of false opinions with regard to the Blessed Eucharist, and to avoid any other ill effects that may follow. (emphasis added)[10]

Four countries—Holland, Belgium, West Germany, and France—the only four countries to have previously and disobediently allowed Communion in the hand (the "contrary usage") were all given a green light for the irreverent practice, thereby rewarding disobedience through acquiescence. The right to do so was an "indult," which could be canceled at the pleasure of Rome. Every other nation was to respect reception on the tongue, for Paul VI had instructed in the same document that, "in view of the gravity of the matter and the force of the arguments put forward, the Holy Father has decided not to change the existing way of administering Holy Communion to the faithful."[11]

Memoriale Domini included a litany of instructions delineated for the protection of Communion on the tongue as "the most fruitful." In hindsight, based on historical experience, it appears possible that these affirmations might simply have been Roman window dressing; all of them were categorically ignored and quickly discarded by Rome, an appalling development widely embraced by victorious progressives. In effect, most of the defenses raised in *Memoriale Domini*—specifically enumerated to encourage Communion on the tongue—never surfaced again;

the erected parapets were inconsequential. Rome rubber stamped its approval on every application seeking the fateful indult.

As a result, the irreverent manner of reception quietly spread around the globe.

In February 1970, a mere nine months after the release of *Memoriale Domini*, the indult was granted to both South Africa and Canada. In 1971, it went to Rhodesia, and to Zambia in 1974. Over the next few years came New Zealand, Australia, England and Wales, Papua and New Guinea, Ireland, and Pakistan. In not one of those countries was "contrary usage" the prevailing manner of reception—not even close.

That applied to the United States, which in 1977 was next up. How much of a battle would it be for then-Archbishop Joseph Bernardin, the powerful head of the NCCB, to push the innovation through?

Bernardin had initiated two previous unsuccessful attempts to introduce Communion in the hand, failing in both 1975 and 1976. Then, from May 3–5, 1977, at the General Meeting in Chicago, the NCCB's own minutes capture the drama:

> The agenda for the meeting was presented by Archbishop Bernardin. He noted that the Administrative Committee had placed the question of Communion in the hand in the open session of the meeting. Bishop John Mugavero (Brooklyn) moved that the agenda be approved. Bishop Romeo Blanchette (Joliet) and five other bishops objected, and proposed in writing the following amendment to the agenda item concerning Communion in the hand:
>
> I. A written vote by the Ordinaries as to whether the contrary usage, that of placing Holy Communion in the hand, prevails in this country as is required by the Instruction on the Manner of Administering Holy Communion [*Memoriale Domini*] of the Sacred Congregation of Divine Worship, 29 May 1969, before a vote is taken to see if a national conference of bishops is to seek a dispensation from the common usage;

> II. and, that the agenda be adopted with the stipulation that the vote on Communion in the hand be taken only if the vote mentioned above is affirmative.[12]

Bishop Blanchette also moved that the amendment be adopted by a written ballot. He wanted to make clear to the assembled American bishops that Pope Paul VI specifically stated they could not vote on the matter without first establishing that Communion in the hand was the "prevailing" custom in the United States. Nonetheless, a show of hands declared that Blanchette's motion was out of order.

The American bishops, well aware of Bernardin's wishes, ignored the "contrary usage" requirement. Although the vote fell short of the required two-thirds of all *de jure* members, a polling of absentee bishops carried the day.

Joseph Bernardin and his followers had conquered a tradition that might have been 1,400 years old, one that was practiced at the first Catholic Mass ever offered in America. In May 1977, Communion in the hand was formally introduced into the United States. Soon, Bernardin's boys—clerics advanced to bishoprics and key positions within the American bishops' bureaucracy, serving major dioceses all across the nation—force-fed Communion in the hand on a Church and its faithful that had shown no interest in the innovation whatsoever.

Blanchette, who obviously knew an end run when he saw one, expressed his dissatisfaction:

> What bothers me is that in the minds of many it will seem that disobedience is being rewarded. And that troubles me because if people persist in being disobedient—and that is used as a reason for changing the discipline—then we're very close to chaos or what I would call selective obedience, which is no obedience at all.[13]

All the protestations of Paul VI, all of his prescient warnings against the dangers of Communion in the hand, were tossed to the wayside. The unfortunate day would come when, in many parishes across America and around the world, every single communicant would receive Holy Communion in the hand, apparently without a second thought. One way or the other, at one time or another, all the fears openly expressed by Paul VI became reality.

After a heroic and very public battle with pancreatic cancer, Joseph Cardinal Bernardin died in 1996. Today, close to two decades later, his legacy lives on.

Neither Joseph Bernardin, nor Paul VI—nor, for that matter, thousands of progressives who welcomed similar beliefs—ever imagined they would engulf the worldwide Church and its faithful people in a massive new eucharistic storm of denial, disbelief, confusion, and indifferentism.

No one, it appears, had any idea.

1 The following year, he would be John Cardinal Dearden.

2 Thomas F. Roeser, "A Letter from Chicago: Is America's Greatest Archdiocese Really in Decline?" *Crisis Magazine*, July 1, 1994, http://www.crisismagazine.com/1994/a-letter-from-chicago-is-americas-greatest-archdiocese-really-in-decline.

3 Eugene Kennedy, *Cardinal Bernardin: Easing Conflicts—and Battling for the Soul of American Catholicism* (Los Angeles: Bonus Books, 1989), 149.

4 George Weigel, "The End of the Bernardin Era: The Rise, Dominance, and Decline of a Culturally Accommodating Catholicism," *First Things*, February 2011, http://www.firstthings.com/article/2011/01/the-end-of-the-bernardin-era.

5 Ibid.

6 Catholic advocates of homosexuality and same-sex marriage immediately recognized the value of this innovative mantra. Both quickly adopted the concept of what, heretofore, was sinful behavior, now conveniently falling under the heading of a "civil liberty" and therefore worthy of acceptance.

7 Joseph Cardinal Bernardin, "A Consistent Ethic of Life: An American-Catholic Dialogue," Lecture, Fordham University, December 6, 1983, 149, http://www.hnp.org/publications/hnpfocus/BConsistentEthic1983.pdf.

8 Joe Sobran, "The 'Seamless Garment' Revisited," August 16, 2005, http://www.sobran.com/columns/2005/050816.shtml.

9 Kennedy, *Cardinal Bernardin*, 132.

10 Sacred Congregation for Divine Worship, *Memoriale Domini: Instruction on the Manner of Distributing Holy Communion*, May 29, 1969, http://www.ewtn.com/library/curia/cdwmemor.htm.

11 Ibid.

12 National Conference of Catholic Bishops, General Meeting: Minutes, May 3–5, 1977.

13 "Bishop Blanchette: A Clear Call for Obedience," National Catholic Register, June 12, 1977.

CHAPTER NINE

Emerging Innovations

The Second Vatican Council wasn't the offensive that threatened to derail the Church. It was merely a convenient vehicle that appeared at the perfect historical time. The opportunities it presented to radicalize the liturgy, as well as the Church at large, were unprecedented.

In all likelihood, neo-modernists couldn't believe their luck. They simply jumped on board to wreak liturgical havoc on a global basis.

Latin was all but wiped out, even though the Council documents called for its continued use. The priest turned to face the people, effectively and symbolically showing his back to God, despite the fact that Vatican II never even suggested the innovation. Communion in the hand? Not a word in any document anywhere. Extraordinary ministers handling the Bread of Life? Impossible. A plentitude of innovations appeared, one after another, and rocked the Church like nothing ever had.

After decades of waiting in the wings, modernism's turn had come. The perfect eucharistic storm had formed, and foremost in its cross hairs was transubstantiation and the Real Presence, God Himself, the primary delineators between Roman Catholicism and Protestantism.

Protestantism, of course, totally denied the Real Presence. The reformers refused to acknowledge its divinity. They declared it to be nothing more than a symbol. They denied the sacrament of Holy Orders. They stood to receive in the hand. They refused to kneel or genuflect to bread.

Bread, after all, is bread.

Then, in the 1960s, history repeated itself, this time in Roman Catholic churches all around the world.

The strategic offense began subtly enough—*strategic* because the changes didn't come from nowhere: no one had requested them, they were completely unexpected, and relatively few people had expressed interest or wanted them. Nevertheless, they openly came and conquered in a breathlessly short time. Doubtless, these sequential innovations were thoughtfully planned.

Fifteen hundred years of tradition would go out the window in less than a single decade. Roman Catholic faithful, clergy and laity alike, had no idea they were about to be engulfed by a new eucharistic storm destined to surpass the tsunami of the Protestant Reformation, with far more damaging results.

There must have been offensive goals, and we can define and measure the success of those goals by the known results.

The Real Presence had to be minimized, subjugated, and trivialized. Roman Catholics had to learn to doubt, then choose to deny, just as their Protestant cousins had done a few hundred years earlier. Most critical of all was the virtual annihilation of reverence; ultimately, if necessary at all, a slight nod of the head would suffice.

Just as in the Reformation, these initiatives were accomplished not from dangerous enemies operating outside of the Church, but from treacherous progressives within, safely operating from comfortable positions of power and authority. Step by deliberate step, the Bread of Life was woven into a symbolic Protestant meal. Over the next fifty years or so, a significant percentage of us would learn to reject the Church's dogma on the Real Presence.[1] Without question, this was, and is, catastrophic for the Church and millions of endangered souls, especially those who walked out the doors never to return.

It has been estimated that, since 1965, up to a third of all Roman Catholics surrendered their faith worldwide. Michael Voris, the founder of ChurchMilitant.TV, estimates 30 million souls walked away in the United States alone. In 2008, the Pew Forum on Religion and

Public Life issued a Religious Landscape Survey stating that one in ten adult Americans is an ex-Catholic. The report noted that if fallen-away Catholics were a denomination, they would represent the second largest denomination in America after Roman Catholicism.[2]

No matter how large the tragic number of deserted souls might be globally, the alarm bells failed to ring—in Rome, or in the vast majority of local dioceses and parishes, wherever they might be. The alarm bells did not ring then, nor do they ring now. One has to wonder: *Why*?

A telltale gust of wind appeared on April 25, 1964. The words used for the distribution of Holy Communion were changed. *Corpus Christi* and the response *Amen* were substituted for the traditional *Corpus Domini nostri Jesu Christi custodiat animam tuam in vitam aeternam. Amen.*[3] It was quicker, shorter, easier, more convenient. Few demurred.

A few months later, on November 21st, the eucharistic fast of three hours was reduced to one hour with the promulgation of *Attentis Multarum.*[4] It would be a tiny sacrifice, easily manageable, with marginal impact. No problem.

The following year, 1965, a major storm front opened in Europe. As we have seen, Protestant reformers invented sixteenth-century-style Communion in the hand to show the Eucharist was merely bread; to destroy the dogma that the Real Presence was the Body, Blood, Soul, and Divinity of God Himself; and to eradicate any thought that a priest's anointed hands had the power to consecrate bread and wine into the Body and Blood of Christ.

Four hundred years later, in progressive minds, with any luck—and without the distraction of transubstantiation and the Real Presence—there would be very little difference between Catholics and our Protestant brothers and sisters. Perhaps, in time, we could all share in just "one Church."

Was Communion in the hand a derivative of Vatican II? Although the practice was often promoted under the guise of being an "authentic" liturgical development mandated by the Council, Communion in the hand was not an organic development, was not mandated by the Second Vatican Council, and shows complete defiance and contempt for centuries of Catholic teaching and practice. Notably, in all sixteen documents of the Council, there is not a single record regarding Communion in the hand, nor was it ever mentioned during any of the Council debates.

That failed to discourage progressives. Ignoring up to 1,400 years of history and tradition, European priests—together with a handful of bishops and cardinals—flaunted the law of the Church to openly disobey Paul VI. Many Catholics were horrified; the irreverence went against everything Catholics had been taught. After all, we believed that it was sacrilegious for anyone but a priest (and, historically, a deacon) to touch the Sacred Host. We were also well aware that some of our saints had died protecting the Holy Eucharist from non-believers.

In fairness to His Holiness, Paul VI attempted to block Communion in the hand at the onset:

> The Holy Father . . . does not consider it opportune that the sacred Particle be distributed in the hand and later consumed in different manners by the faithful, and therefore, he vehemently exhorts [that] the Conference offer the opportune resolutions so that the traditional manner of communicating be restored throughout the world.[5]

The pope was rebuffed by headstrong cardinals, bishops, priests, and laypeople.

For Rome, the disobedience presented a challenge that had to be addressed. Or was it, perhaps for some, an opportunity that couldn't be missed? Pope Paul VI appointed a committee—Consilium ad exsequendam Constitutionem de Sacra Liturgia—to direct the on-going liturgical renewal. On July 30, 1968, the Consilium issued a document admitting that the problem of Communion in the hand is not exclusively liturgical, but has strong pastoral and, even more, psychological consequences. Worship and veneration of the Blessed Sacrament, as well as the very faith in the sacrament, will be not a little affected . . . *unless the transition from the traditional way of receiving to the new one is gradually and carefully prepared for.*[6] (emphasis added)

For Paul VI, the obligation to condemn the irreverent practice arrived. One word from His Holiness and it would have been shelved, quickly and without question, perhaps for another few hundred years. Yet the Consilium's written words turned out to be terribly prophetic.

Instead of forbidding the innovation, the pope instead chose to conduct a vote on the matter—a highly unusual event with no historical precedent. Two thousand bishops across the globe were polled:

- Fifty-nine percent of bishops said the laity of their diocese would not accept the new practice.
- Sixty-two percent of bishops did not want to see the practice begin in their diocese.
- Sixty-six percent of the bishops didn't think the practice was worth addressing.[7]

The English Church hierarchy warned that a decision of this magnitude would cast doubt on the Real Presence. Argentine bishops found the idea offensive. The Italians expressed concern about scandal and further sacrileges. African bishops worried about the possibility of sorcerers and witch doctors obtaining hosts for evil ceremonies. Protests came in from across the globe.[8]

In 1969, Pope Paul VI decided on a striking compromise with his wayward bishops, one that would avoid the unpleasantness of censure. Given "the gravity of the matter," the pope refused to authorize Communion in the hand. Instead, he offered an *indult*, an exception to the law, under certain conditions:

> First, an indult could not be given to a country *in which Communion in the hand was not an already established practice*; (emphasis added)

Second, the bishops in countries where it was established must approve of the practice by a secret vote and with a two-thirds majority.

And third, the Holy See set down seven regulations concerning Communion in the hand; failure to maintain these regulations could result in the loss of the indult. The first three of these regulations concerned respecting the laity who continue the traditional practice, maintaining the laity's proper respect of the Eucharist, and strengthening the laity's faith in the Real Presence.[9]

Memoriale Domini authorized Communion in the hand only to those countries where it had come into common use, and whose bishops saw fit to approve it. For those four countries that already adopted the practice, the pope warned:

> A change in a matter of such moment, based on a most ancient and venerable tradition, does not merely affect discipline. It carries certain dangers with it which may arise from the new manner of administering Holy Communion: the danger of a loss of reverence for the august sacrament of the altar, of profanation, of adulterating the true doctrine.[10]

Paul VI understood perfectly. He also defended and encouraged the existing practice of receiving Communion on the tongue:

> From the returns it is clear that the vast majority of bishops believe that the present discipline should not be changed, and that if it were, the change would be offensive to the sentiments and the spiritual culture of these bishops and of many of the faithful.
>
> Therefore, taking into account the remarks and the advice of those whom the Holy Spirit has placed to rule over the Churches, in view

> of the gravity of the matter and the force of the arguments put forward, the Holy Father has decided not to change the existing way of administering Holy Communion to the faithful.

The Apostolic See therefore emphatically urges bishops, priests and laity to obey carefully the law which is still valid and which has again been confirmed. It urges them to take account of the judgment given by the majority of Catholic bishops, of the rite now in use in the liturgy, of the common good of the Church.[11]

Paradoxically, he authorized the irreverent practice under very specific conditions, and then stated that it could be offensive to the faithful, warning that it could lead to a loss of reverence, of profanation, and of adulterating the true doctrine. Although his instructions were often contradictory, truer words were never written.

Today, there is hardly a Novus Ordo Mass anywhere in the Western world in which the majority of the laity—and in many churches, every communicant—doesn't receive in the hand while standing (a few exceptions noted). Does that mean the pope's instructions are nothing more than empty words to be universally ignored? Decidedly, the answer is yes. The directives of Pope Paul VI, the author of *Memoriale Domini*, are very specific. They are also categorically rejected at every level of the Church.

Before the heady decade came to a close, the progressives had one final initiative to implement, and it was a fateful one.

On November 30, 1969, Pope Paul VI's *Novus Ordo* Missal became mandatory in the Roman Rite, the First Sunday of Advent of that year. *Sitting* was now the recommended posture for thanksgiving after Holy Communion, for both the priest and the congregation. No longer was the priest required to hold together the thumb and forefinger of both hands after the consecration. A tradition spanning at least a thousand years, required to avoid all profane contact, was obliterated overnight. The priest was also freed from the obligation to purify his fingers at the altar during the ablutions.

For the faithful, this latest volley also introduced a shocking novelty: the pious Western custom of kneeling to receive the Eucharist was abolished. Suddenly, kneeling to receive God Himself was a quaint custom from the past. Standing would be the new norm.

The altar rails were declared useless. Altar rails separated the sanctuary, our Holy of Holies, from the body of the church. The sanctuary is where the sacrifice of Christ takes place in the Holy Sacrifice of the Mass, and where Christ remains in the tabernacle in His abiding presence in the Most Blessed Sacrament. It was only secondarily that the altar rail was utilized for the Communion of the faithful.

None of that mattered. The altar rails quickly fell, universally, often smashed to pieces, in a strange, surrealistic mirror image of what transpired during the Reformation. History repeated itself once more.

The sixteenth-century reformers, had they known, would surely have been ecstatic! Literally standing in their place were the neo-modernists, and one can only imagine their joy. A major eucharistic tsunami had triumphed, perhaps beyond the wildest dreams of its innovators. The storm was destined to go worldwide. Within just a few short years, tens of millions of Catholics would walk out the doors, most never to return.

Closing in on half a century later, the fall-out continues.

1 The percentage of people who reject the teaching of the Real Presence ranges from a minimum of 19% to a maximum of 70%. The well-known *New York Times* survey from the early 1990s that declared a 70% rejection of belief in the Real Presence is widely considered to be fatally flawed. A more recent poll, the 2011 "Catholics in America" survey, declares that a minority of Catholics—just 46%—believe in the dogma of the Real Presence. See the following links: http://forums.ssrc.org/ndsp/2013/06/24/the-catholic-17-and-modernitys-other-ways; see also Abp. Michael J. Sheehan, "Is the Eucharist Really Christ's Body and Blood?" https://www.catholicculture.org/culture/library/view.cfm?recnum=1340.

2 The Pew Forum, "U.S. Religions Landscape Survey," February 2008, http://religions.pewforum.org/pdf/report-religious-landscape-study-full.pdf.

3 "May the Body of our Lord Jesus Christ preserve your soul unto life everlasting."

4 Geoffrey Hull, *The Banished Heart: Origins of Heteropraxis in the Catholic Church* (London: Bloomsbury/T&T Clark, 2010), 9.
5 Letter of the Consilium to Bernard Cardinal Alfrink, Archbishop of Utrecht, Netherlands, October 12, 1965.
6 Hull, *The Banished Heart*, 14.
7 Sacred Congregation for Divine Worship, *Memoriale Domini*.
8 Hull, *The Banished Heart*, 14–15.
9 Sacred Congregation for Divine Worship, *Memoriale Domini*.
10 Ibid.
11 Ibid.

CHAPTER TEN

Damage Control

Without a shadow of a doubt, the 1960s was a triumphant era for progressives. No one can deny their worldwide success, nor the serious impact they had on the Church. Even so, their journey of "renewal"—their hopes and dreams to radicalize the Church and challenge its core beliefs—had just begun.

The future beckoned, and it was promising.

The first offensive of the new decade commenced on June 29, 1970. The Holy See promulgated *Sacramentali Communione*, allowing the reception of Holy Communion under both species.[1] This was another win for Church progressives, obviously scripted to meet future planned objectives.

Two and a half years later, on January 29, 1973, *Immensae Caritatis* was released. Once again, a major instruction was authored by Paul VI, this one allowing lay people of both sexes to distribute Holy Communion as "extraordinary ministers." *Immensae Caritatis* was a full-blown novelty, contributing to the death knell of reverence and minimizing the station of Holy Orders. Never in the two millennia of the Church had anything remotely similar ever occurred.[2]

There were rules, of course, dictated in *Immensae Caritatis* to guide the faithful. But as we have repeatedly learned, instructions from Paul VI were, and are, emphatically ignored. Here is what His Holiness wrote:

> Local Ordinaries possess the faculty enabling them to permit fit persons, each chosen by name as a special minister, in a given instance

or for a set period or even permanently, to give Communion to themselves and others of the faithful and to carry it to the sick residing at home:

- whenever no priest, deacon, or acolyte is available;
- whenever the same ministers are impeded from administering Communion because of another pastoral ministry, ill health, or old age;
- whenever the number of faithful wishing to receive Communion is so great that the celebration of Mass or the giving of Communion outside Mass would take too long.[3]

The instruction further stipulates that:

Since these faculties are granted only for the spiritual good of the faithful and for cases of genuine necessity priests are to remember that they are not thereby excused from the task of distributing the Eucharist to the faithful who legitimately request it, and especially from taking and giving it to the sick.[4]

Similar to the vague documents that emerged from Vatican II, the wording in *Immensae caritatis* was ambiguous and imprecise. The third stipulation permitting extraordinary ministers to distribute Communion in cases where Mass "would take too long" is a good example. Would that be five, fifteen, or fifty-five minutes? Who decides?

No one had any idea, but neo-modernists recognized an opportunity and seized the moment. In fact, their on-going success highlights the vast number of their brethren operating in untold numbers of parishes and dioceses worldwide. Seemingly overnight, churches everywhere were flooded with liturgical lay ministers. A veritable army invaded the sanctuary, our revered Holy of Holies: enthusiastic, eager volunteers reading the new Responsorial Psalms, conducting the Prayers of the Faithful, and even distributing Holy Communion (extraordinary ministers). The sanctuary suddenly erupted into a center stage, populated by lay people occupying sacred space formerly reserved for those with Holy Orders.

Apparently, it never occurred to anyone that, just by being there, lay ministers were trivializing the sanctified, holy altar of God in the eyes of the laity. Nor did they consider the subtle impact and minimization irreverence had on the sacrament of Holy Orders.

The storm path widened, taking an ever greater toll as it continued to batter down the barriers of reverence. The fall-out continued.

"Ordinary" means a priest or deacon. "Extraordinary" means someone other than a priest or deacon, and that person is to be used on limited occasions. The practice of distributing Holy Communion is reserved for extraordinary circumstances, and not for everyday usage. Thus, the abuse of Communion in the hand was mirrored by laypeople who—in the vast majority of cases—should rarely be allowed in the sanctuary, rarely touch the sacred vessels, and rarely open the tabernacle, except under truly extraordinary circumstances.

What happened, of course, is that, in the ensuing decades, there followed a long history of liturgical excesses and abuses: The exception became the norm.

It soon became evident that some cardinals, bishops, priests, deacons, nuns, and laity alike were globally discounting the instructions of Paul VI. Nonetheless, for the Church's progressive army, this was a time for celebration. No longer would the Real Presence be a stumbling block between Roman Catholicism and our Protestant brothers and sisters, for the simple reason that the dogma was rarely taught. Progressives had discovered the most effective way to destroy transubstantiation and the Real Presence: *unconditionally ignore both, never mentioning their antiquated, consequential words from the pulpit, or anywhere else . . . ever.* (Exceptions, again, noted, but they were few and far between.)

Message received, loud and clear.

In February 1980, Pope Saint John Paul II issued *Dominicae Cenae,* writing in part,

> [C]ases of deplorable lack of respect toward the Eucharistic species have been reported, cases which are imputable not only to the individuals guilty of such behavior, but also to the pastors of the Church who have not been vigilant enough regarding the attitude of the faithful towards the Eucharist.[5]

Progressives yawned. Year after year, the abuses mounted across the globe. Catholics continued to melt away. The children of baby boomers deserted in shockingly large numbers (and continue to do so). In time, parishes would begin closing or "consolidating."

To address the ongoing problem, in August 1997, the Vatican issued the instruction "On Certain Questions Regarding the Collaboration of the Non-Ordained Faithful in the Sacred Ministry of Priest." In Article 8, the Church once again clarified that the use of Extraordinary Ministers of Holy Communion should only be utilized "at eucharistic celebrations where there are particularly large numbers of the faithful and which would be excessively prolonged because of an insufficient number of ordained ministers to distribute Holy Communion."[6] Nothing changed.

In 2002, Pope Saint John Paul II warned against the tendency to "clericalise the laity," which he said had resulted from false interpretations of the Second Vatican Council. When greeting a group of bishops from western Brazil in Rome for their *ad limina* visit, the Pope said there is a "confusion of functions," which originates in erroneous theological interpretations.[7]

"Among the objectives of the liturgical reform, established by Vatican Council II, was the need to have all the faithful participate in liturgical ceremonies," the Holy Father told the bishops. "However, in practice, in the years following the Council, in order to fulfill this desire, the confusion of functions in regard to the priestly ministry and role of the laity was arbitrarily extended," he said. Symptoms of this confusion are "the indiscriminate and common recitation of the Eucharistic Prayer," "homilies given by lay people," and the *"distribution of Communion by the laity"* (emphasis added). These "grave abuses often originated in doctrinal errors, especially in regard to the nature of the liturgy, of the common priesthood of Christians, of the vocation and mission of the laity, but also in regard to the ordained ministry of priests," the Pope stressed.[8]

Finally, in 2004, neo-modernists blanched as the Holy See acted. The Congregation for Divine Worship and the Discipline of the Sacraments promulgated the instruction *Redemptionis Sacramentum*, which clarified certain matters regarding the Eucharist. It should have been a blockbuster:

> It is not possible to be silent about the abuses, even quite grave ones, against the nature of the Liturgy and the Sacraments as well as the tradition and the authority of the Church, which in our day not infrequently plague liturgical celebrations in one ecclesial environment or another. In some places the perpetration of liturgical abuses has become almost habitual, a fact which obviously cannot be allowed and must cease.[9]
>
> The Mystery of the Eucharist 'is too great for anyone to permit himself to treat it according to his own whim, so that its sacredness and its universal ordering would be obscured'. On the contrary, anyone who acts thus by giving free rein to his own inclinations, even if he is a Priest, injures the substantial unity of the Roman Rite, which ought to be vigorously preserved, and becomes responsible for actions that are in no way consistent with the hunger and thirst for the living God that is experienced by the people today. Nor do such actions serve authentic pastoral care or proper liturgical renewal; instead, they deprive Christ's faithful of their patrimony and their heritage. For arbitrary actions are not conducive to true renewal, but are detrimental to the right of Christ's faithful to a liturgical celebration that is an expression of the Church's life in accordance

> with her tradition and discipline. In the end, they introduce elements of distortion and disharmony into the very celebration of the Eucharist, which is oriented in its own lofty way and by its very nature to signifying and wondrously bringing about the communion of divine life and the unity of the People of God.[10]

Paragraph 88 states that it is "the priest celebrant's responsibility" to distribute Holy Communion, perhaps assisted by other priests or deacons who are present. "Only when there is a necessity may extraordinary ministers assist the Priest celebrant in accordance with the norm of law."[11]

Paragraph 91 defends the right to kneel during reception: "Therefore, it is not licit to deny Holy Communion to any of Christ's faithful solely on the grounds, for example, that the person wishes to receive the Eucharist kneeling or standing."[12]

Paragraph 151 explains that EMHCs are to be used "only out of true necessity" and when they are used, *"special urgent prayers of intercession should be multiplied that the Lord may soon send a priest for the service of the community"*[13] (emphasis added).

Paragraph 157 teaches that, "if there is a sufficient number of ordinary ministers present, then EMHCs should not be used."[14]

Sadly, bad habits are hard to break. Post-Vatican II progressives have proven time and again that rules and regulations from Rome, the very stipulations that faithful Catholics rely on, can be changed, modified, or distorted at the wave of a hand.

Few Catholics have ever heard of *Redemptionis Sacramentum*, and its instructions are rarely taught to the laity. At many churches around the globe, the veritable army is still in place. It is almost inexplicable that anything impacting the Real Presence—the very heart and soul of Roman Catholicism—wouldn't be unveiled from the pulpits and taught to the laity everywhere. Nonetheless, the average Catholic has never heard of these dictums, has no idea what they mean, and, frankly, doesn't appear to be overly concerned.

That applies to EMHCs who should rarely be in the sanctuary or distributing Holy Communion, and to the laity who should never be receiving Communion in the hand, especially from an EMHC. Few of us have been properly formed because progressives have no desire whatsoever in reigniting the dreaded word "reverence," which has been all but eradicated.

Many who argue for receiving Communion in the hand from an Extraordinary Minister of Holy Communion do so because "it is permitted." That is, unfortunately, true, but the Lord's response to the Pharisees when they questioned divorce is worth considering:[15] "They said to him, 'Why then did Moses command one to give a certificate of divorce, and to put her away?' He said to them, 'For your hardness of heart Moses allowed you to divorce your wives, but from the beginning it was not so'" (Matthew 19:7–8).

Are we suffering from hard-heartedness, or are we simply too proud to humble ourselves by kneeling and receiving on the tongue from a priest? Or is this merely a matter of believing it should be "our way"?

Our Catholic liturgy is well structured and highly ordered, because God is the God of order who created an ordered world. The sacred liturgy is about the correct and orderly worship and adoration of God; it should never be about what we want or how we "feel." (How has that worked out for Protestantism?) The Mass is about Jesus Christ, the eternal Son of God. It is not about us, and never has been.[16]

In essence, the rights to participate in damaging innovations are nothing more than willful illusions, subterfuge embraced by progressives and their unwitting followers, many of whom have no idea what reality should be. As in every other arena of life, the refusal to separate illusion from reality frequently spawns catastrophic consequences.

One regrettable example over the past few decades has been First Communion, an early, primary casualty of the present eucharistic storm. At the majority of Novus Ordo churches, almost every child—and in some cases every one of the First Communicants—receives Communion in the hand while standing. The few parents who insist on

Communion on the tongue from a priest frequently discover that they are in for a serious battle. Kneeling? Not on your life. (Again, exceptions noted.) This is wrong on so many levels it is almost unbelievable.[17]

Here is a recent posting online from the mother of a First Communicant, representative of multiple emails and postings received over the past few years at www.Communion-in-the-hand.org:

> When one of my eight children was making her First Communion I thought she would receive on the tongue as I had instructed her, to preserve in my family this sign of ultimate reverence for Our Lord in His Blessed Sacrament. You can imagine my heartbreak and shock when against my wishes, she put out her hand as all the other children were doing. I asked afterwards how this had happened and was told that one mother had complained that all the children should be in unity of how they receive . . . so since she wanted her child to receive in the hand it was changed at the last minute for all by that one complaint. Still heartbroken over that lack of respect taught to my daughter on her First Communion Day.[18]

Witness anything remotely like this and know that progressives are uncomfortably close, and very, very much in control.

Based on history over the past few decades, we know that—barring unforeseen events—the majority of these little children will walk away from the Church at some point in their young lives, deny belief in the Real Presence, whether they acknowledge or realize it or not, and abandon the faith. In truth, their parents may very well beat them out the door. Statistically, at least 80 percent or more of Catholic parents no longer attend Sunday Mass regularly, and not a few of these First Communion parents will rarely, if ever, be seen again.

What chance do their children have?

Is it possible to receive Communion in the hand reverently, while standing, often from an unnecessary EMHC? Putting aside common sense and the ignored instructions from Rome, most serious

Catholics would probably agree that the answer, for them, is "yes." However, once reverence exists with its positive and elevating influence on the consciousness of the faithful, it is obvious that withdrawing that reverence sends a clear, negative signal, and it surely has: For some, since reverence was never required, there is nothing sacred present that commands reverence or even respect. As a result, the example set by so many continues to spawn confusion, indifferentism, denial, and disbelief. Ultimately, the toll includes consequential fall-out at the vast majority of Catholic churches around the globe.

Nonetheless, without accepting irreverence at any level, it is important to note that we cannot and should not judge the intentions of others receiving Holy Communion. They clearly receive in this manner because the Church unfortunately allows and sometimes even encourages it. We are responsible only for ourselves.

Thus, each of us must ask: Is irreverence really worth the price? Can I afford not to recognize and revere the sacredness of the Real Presence by my thoughts, words, and actions?

In Alice von Hildebrand's *Introduction to the Philosophy of Religion*, she wrote:

> Sacredness is such an essential element of man's religious life that it can be considered to be a barometer for the vitality of a particular religion. The moment the sense for the sacred diminishes, it is a sure sign that the faithful of that particular religion are becoming secularized—that they have lost the sense for the things that are above.

For decades, a number of priests and bishops around the world, deeply entrenched in the eucharistic storm, cajoled and even ordered the faithful to stand while receiving Holy Communion. Never mind that Catholics were receiving God Himself: Some of the reasons presented were that kneeling is "divisive," it "slowed things down," or "we could trip someone." (*Redemptionis Sacramentum*, of course, was totally ignored.)

In the United States, that changed with the 2010 version of the USCCB's General Instruction of the Roman Missal (GIRM):

> 160. The norm established for the Dioceses of the United States of America is that Holy Communion is to be received standing, unless an individual member of the faithful wishes to receive Communion while kneeling.[19]

This was an unheralded change. In America, we could once again kneel to receive, but for some reason this was never read to us from the pulpit. Even today, most Catholics have no idea.

Living in darkness and denial isn't particularly pleasant, but our progressive friends couldn't appear happier. By studying the achieved results, it is easy to draw the conclusion that their numbers are vast and operating at every level of the global Church. All of them assuredly count themselves fortunate to be on the winning side of history.

Who are the losers in this titanic battle to annihilate reverence? Until now, they have been faithful Catholics, trying desperately to live in the light of Christ and Tradition, and that includes clergy and laity alike. Their numbers are not insignificant, either. Better yet, many of them have awoken from a deep and lasting slumber that has spanned nearly half a century. They're awake, they are watching, and they are learning. Moreover, ever-increasing numbers of them are voting with their feet, and taking their families with them, in a search for reverent Novus Ordo Masses, Traditional Latin Mass churches, or Byzantine liturgies.

The road ahead is illuminated by fifty years of systemic failure. This present eucharistic storm, it turns out, was an incalculable disaster, replete with on-going collateral damage.

All of us are paying a steep price.

1 Sacred Congregation for Divine Worship, *Sacramentali Communione*, http://www.ewtn.com/library/CURIA/CDWBOTH.HTM.
2 Sacred Congregation of the Sacraments, *Immensae Caritatis*, http://www.ewtn.com/library/CURIA/CDWIMCAR.htm.
3 Ibid.
4 Ibid.
5 Pope Saint John Paul II, *Dominicae Cenae*, http://www.vatican.va/holy_father/john_paul_ii/letters/documents/hf_jp-ii_let_24021980_dominicae-cenae_en.html.
6 Congregation for the Clergy, "On Certain Questions Regarding the Collaboration of the Non-Ordained Faithful in the Sacred Ministry of Priest" (Vatican City: Libreria Editrice Vaticana, 1997), http://www.vatican.va/roman_curia/pontifical_councils/laity/documents/rc_con_interdic_doc_15081997_en.html.
7 "Pope Warns Against 'Clericalising' the Laity," *Catholic News*, September 25, 2002, http://cathnews.acu.edu.au/209/146.php.
8 Ibid.
9 Congregation for Divine Worship and the Discipline of the Sacraments, *Redemptionis Sacramentum*, http://www.vatican.va/roman_curia/congregations/ccdds/documents/rc_con_ccdds_doc_20040423_redemptionis-sacramentum_en.html.
10 Ibid.,11.
11 Ibid., 88.
12 Ibid., 91.
13 Ibid., 151.
14 Ibid., 157.
15 Brian Williams, "A Sign of Adoration," *Liturgy Guy*, November 25, 2013, http://liturgyguy.com/2013/11/25/a-sign-of-adoration.
16 Facebook commentary, December 10, 2013, http://communion-in-the-hand.org.
17 The excuse most often provided seems to be "unity," but there is little or no unification around reverence and tradition. Why?
18 A posting from Catholic mother MPM, February 4, 2013, https://www.facebook.com/pages/Communion-In-The-Hand/166735166736513?fref=ts.
19 *Redemptionis Sacramentum*, 91. I didn't research other countries, but this change was definitely a response to Rome's instructions.

CHAPTER ELEVEN

Playing the Obedience Card

Roma locuta est! "Rome has spoken!" Saint Catherine of Siena couldn't have agreed more when she wrote

> Oh! How sweet and glorious is this virtue of obedience, which contains all the other virtues! Because it is born of charity, and on it the rock of the holy Faith is founded; it is a queen, and he who espouses it knows no evil, but only peace and rest.

Faithful Roman Catholics rightfully cherish obedience, and always have. It is the moral virtue shared by Catholics universally, part of our heritage, bred into our hearts and minds. We were raised on obedience from childhood; it set us apart from the world, and we knew it.

Few of us had any idea that the potential for using obedience improperly has never been overlooked by the enemy within—and without.

In the 1960s, it was obedience that enabled the sweeping changes in the Church, and *disobedience* that empowered all the radical innovations to follow. As the innovations unfolded one after another, we were often reminded to be obedient, that Rome knew best, that obedience filtered from the Pope all the way down to our local parish priest, then to each of us.

This was the secret weapon deployed by progressives, effectively turned against the faithful with deadly accuracy. Suddenly, unexpectedly, obedience required us to believe and accept what had once been unbelievable and unacceptable. There was nowhere to hide.

From 1965 on, as the innovations came fast and furious, a vast, eager army of neo-modernists were waiting with bated breath. Each one was anxious to play his or her unique role in the radicalization of the liturgy and Church practices, and the annihilation of tradition. The innovators were in place, randomly integrated in key positions throughout the Church hierarchy, cascading all the way down to innumerable local parishes.

Since most of us had no idea of their very existence, we were blissfully unaware that *they* had no use for obedience. Thus, progressives interpreted, revised, and deployed the documents of Vatican II—together with *Memoriale Domini* and *Immensae Caritatis*—to reflect their own personal agendas. Those agendas could be as varied and toxic as one could imagine—from person to person, church to church, diocese to diocese.

Supporters of sweeping changes in the life of the Church have always claimed there were no ambiguities in the documents of Vatican II, only in the interpretation of them. Then, unexpectedly, on April 11, 2013, well-known liberal Cardinal Walter Kasper stated that ambiguities were *deliberately* inserted into Vatican II documents, leaving them subject to a multitude of interpretations. His comments appeared in the pages of the Vatican's own newspaper, *L'Osservatore Romano*:

> In many places, they had to find compromise formulas, in which, often, the positions of the majority are located immediately next to those of the minority, designed to delimit them. Thus, the conciliar texts themselves have a huge potential for conflict, open the door to a selective reception in either direction.[1]

One doesn't have to search far to see exactly what Cardinal Kasper was referring to. Here, for example, are a couple of excerpts from *Sacrosanctum Concilium*, beginning with a recommendation in its preface: "where necessary, the rites be carefully and thoroughly revised in the light of sound tradition."

This was followed by the exact opposite instruction. The rites should "be given new vigor to meet the circumstances and needs of modern times."[2]

Liturgical innovators—who obviously recognized *carte blanche* when they saw it—must have been more than pleased. From the same document appeared instructions on the question of liturgical language: "Particular law remaining in force, the use of the Latin language is to be preserved in the Latin rites."

This assurance was followed by a roadmap of innovation:

> But since the use of the mother tongue, whether in the Mass, the administration of the sacraments, or other parts of the liturgy, frequently may be of great advantage to the people, the limits of its employment may be extended. This will apply in the first place to the readings and directives, and to some of the prayers and chants, according to the regulations on this matter to be laid down separately in subsequent chapters.
>
> These norms being observed, it is for the competent territorial ecclesiastical authority mentioned in Art. 22, 2, to decide whether, and to what extent, the vernacular language is to be used; their decrees are to be approved, that is, confirmed, by the Apostolic See. And, whenever it seems to be called for, this authority is to consult with bishops of neighboring regions which have the same language.[3]

Good-bye Latin. The historical language of the Church, the immutable language of glory and mystery, didn't stand a chance. Insightfully, Cardinal Kasper went on to say:

> For most Catholics, the developments put in motion by the Council are part of the Church's daily life. But what they are experiencing

> is not the great new beginning nor the springtime of the church, which were expected at that time, but rather a church that has a wintery look, and shows clear signs of crisis.[4]

Cardinal Kasper's words eerily reflected the thoughts from an unhappy Paul VI, who would come to be known as "the sad pope." Four decades earlier, in 1972, reeling from an epidemic of liturgical abuses that followed in the wake of the Council's implementation, the pope stated:

> It was believed that after the Council, there would be a day of sunshine in the history of the Church. There came instead a day of clouds, storm and darkness, of search and uncertainty. Through some fissure, the smoke of Satan has entered the Temple of God.[5]

The 1969 instruction *Memoriale Domini*, allowing Communion in the hand under specific guidelines, was a classic example. As we have seen, the document, authored by Paul VI and released by The Congregation for Divine Worship, began by strongly defending and encouraging Communion on the tongue, stating that this manner of reception was "the most fruitful." Thus, for all the reasons affirmed in *Memoriale Domini*, "the Holy Father has decided not to change the existing way of administering holy communion to the faithful."[6]

None of that mattered in the slightest, for the sequential language in *Memoriale Domini* opened wide the door to irreverent Communion in the hand and the abuses that followed:

> Episcopal conferences should examine matters carefully and should make whatever decisions, by a secret vote and with a two-thirds majority, are needed to regulate matters. Their decisions should be sent to Rome to receive the necessary confirmation. [7]

A "sample letter" was attached, disclosing the specific regulations required by any hierarchy that obtained permission to practice Communion in the hand. One of the instructions reveals the trepidation of its author(s):

> The rite of communion in the hand must be introduced tactfully. In effect, since human attitudes are in question, it is linked with the sensibility of the person receiving communion. It should therefore be introduced gradually, beginning with better-educated and better-prepared groups.[8]

Good-bye, Communion on the tongue, which, within the next few years, was virtually eradicated in many countries around the world. The earlier, critical instructions from Paul VI were unquestionably shunned, then and now.

Cardinal Kasper's unexpected admission should have been a wake-up call for Catholics universally, but much of the Catholic press selectively ignored the revelation.[9] Sadly, the deliberate ambiguities in the Vatican II documents, plus the willful misinterpretations of the same, have led to the dismantling of much of the Church. They effectively created a safe harbor for modernism and its myriad supporters all around the globe and a safety net that still exists today. Progressives were selectively disobedient, and most of them knew it.

The same formula was applied to *Memoriale Domini* and *Immensae Caritatis.*

On the other hand, much of Catholicism—clergy and lay alike—was obedient, unaware of the terrible and lasting price that was to be paid.

Was obedience required by the documents of Vatican II? Millions of words have addressed the question, but one thing is for sure: There was no new dogma released by the Council. Both John XXIII and Paul VI repeatedly declared that Vatican II was a pastoral, non-dogmatic council. In 1988, Cardinal Joseph Ratzinger, the future Pope Benedict XVI, addressed the bishops of Chile. He said, in part:

> The Second Vatican Council has not been treated as a part of the entire living Tradition of the Church, but as an end of Tradition, a new start from zero. The truth is that this particular Council defined no dogma at all, and deliberately chose to remain on a modest level, as a merely pastoral council; and yet many treat it as though it had made itself into a sort of super dogma which takes away the importance of all the rest.[10]

There was, however, dogma—a reiteration of traditional beliefs throughout all of Catholicism, presented and reinforced within the documents, which do indeed require obedience. Progressives ignored them, too.

A tsunami landed in the decade after 1965, a full-frontal attack against the Church, led from progressives in Rome and embraced by a vast number of insiders worldwide. Its seeds originated from the "enlightenment" of the sixteenth century and the darkness of the Protestant Reformation. It evolved into classic modernism and spread like wildfire in the late nineteenth century. In the early twentieth century, Pope St. Pius X valiantly fought it off and, temporarily, beat it into submission. At the end of his pontificate, however, modernism resurfaced with a vengeance.

As the twentieth century developed, and more and more in the Church began to absorb "enlightened" ideas like "tolerance" (indifference) and "the rights of man" (versus the rights of God), support for the dogmatic beliefs of Catholicism slowly but surely eroded.[11] By the late 1950s, the Church had an army of priests, nuns, bishops, and even some cardinals, all of whom embraced a host of modernist themes in an attempt to radicalize the Church. Ultimately, they succeeded beyond anything one could imagine.

A handful of the documents from Vatican II, together with *Memoriale Domini* and *Immensae Caritatis,* empowered a storm front unlike anything the Church has ever experienced. Those seeking to upend and replace the faith took full advantage of every possible interpretation. The result was a de-emphasis or denial of traditional Catholicism and practices, sometimes merely by default, together with innovations that negatively affected the Church and its faithful people. Then the bell of obedience was rung, loudly and continuously. "Social justice" fit neatly into the mold.

In the particular case of *Memoriale Domini,* released four years after the closing of Vatican II, there is nothing to argue about. Yes, thanks to Paul VI and the indult, most of us are allowed—to the detriment of millions of souls—to receive Communion in the hand. However, the document is profoundly clear on how we *should* receive:

> This method of distributing holy communion [on the tongue] must be retained:
>
> - [N]ot merely because it has many centuries of tradition behind it, but especially because it expresses the faithful's reverence for the Eucharist.
> - [I]t is part of that preparation that is needed for the most fruitful reception of the Body of the Lord.
> - [I]n view of the gravity of the matter and the force of the arguments put forward, the Holy Father has decided not to change the existing way of administering holy communion to the faithful.
> - The Apostolic See therefore emphatically urges bishops, priests and laity to obey carefully the law which is still valid and which has again been confirmed.
> - It urges them to take account of the judgment given by the majority of Catholic bishops, of the rite now in use in the liturgy, of the common good of the Church.[12]

Progressives, of course, simply ignored these instructions and confidently forced Communion in the hand. After the obedience card was played, most Catholics dutifully followed.[13]

Now, finally, decades later, truth has emerged. We can and we should receive on the tongue, and—at least here in the United States—we have the right to receive while kneeling. Anyone who blocks either of those manners of reception is being seriously disobedient.

In 2010, Bishop Athanasius Schneider – known for his heroic, worldwide campaign against Communion in the hand – addressed a large group of bishops and cardinals in Rome. He suggested that the time had come for a "Syllabus of Errors" to be published by the Holy Father, specifically to clear up the misinterpretations of the documents of the Second Vatican Council.[14] Those misinterpretations have spawned known consequences, among which is the loss of Catholic identity, without which we willingly squander the sense of what it is to be Catholic. With no idea of what is being surrendered, nominal Catholics freely discard their faith and walk away. The Church shrinks, her sense of self is diminished, her leaders unwilling to recognize, or even admit, that we are in the midst of an unprecedented crisis.

A crisis enabled not by the wonderful moral virtue of obedience, but by its evil twin, disobedience.

1 *L'Osservatore Romano*, April 11, 2013.

2 Second Vatican Council, *Sacrosanctum Concilium*, Introduction, 4, http://www.vatican.va/archive/hist_councils/ii_vatican_council/documents/vat-ii_const_19631204_sacrosanctum-concilium_en.html.

3 Ibid., 36: 1, 2.

4 *L'Osservatore Romano*, April 11, 2013.

5 "Paul VI Saw Liturgical Abuse As Smoke of Satan," http://www.catholicculture.org/news/features/index.cfm?recnum=58473.

6 Sacred Congregation for Divine Worship. *Memoriale Domini.*

7 Ibid.

8 The Instruction was accompanied by a sample of the letter (in French) sent to hierarchies who ask for and are granted permission to introduce the practice of Holy

Communion on the hand. The letter laid down specific regulations, including this one.

9 Michael Voris and ChurchMilitant.TV provided wide coverage of the article. See, e.g., "Deliberately Unclear," Video, June 3, 2013, http://www.youtube.com/watch?v=JFJEUcJ3TOA.

10 Joseph Ratzinger, "Cardinal Ratzinger's Remarks Regarding the Lefebvre Schism," http://www.catholicculture.org/culture/library/view.cfm?recnum=3032.

11 The most tragic example today is the large percentage of misguided Catholics who openly support abortion and same-sex marriage.

12 Sacred Congregation for Divine Worship, *Memoriale Domini*.

13 At Communion-in-the-hand.org, a consistent flow of emails and responses to various postings accuse the editor of being disobedient because the site promotes obedience to *Memoriale Domini*. It appears that the vast majority of Catholics have never read *Memoriale Domini*, have little or no interest in doing so, or fail to understand it. Reading time for the instruction is about five minutes.

14 See Michael Voris, "The Most Reverend Bishop Athanasius Schneider: 'Vatican II Must Be Clarified,'" Interview, June 27, 2013, http://www.youtube.com/watch?v=z8iBeaGeuxw.

CHAPTER TWELVE

Storm Recovery

Fifty years after the commencement of Vatican II, traditional Roman Catholic beliefs and practices are randomly appearing at parishes around the globe, their green shoots routinely posted at www.communion-in-hand.org.

In Phoenix, Arizona, for example, the rector at St. Simon and Jude Cathedral regularly encourages his Novus Ordo flock to receive with reverence on the tongue. (Kneeling is welcome, too.) Across the city at St. Anne's in Mesa, Arizona, kneelers have appeared for the benefit of communicants. In Tiverton, RI, Norwalk, CT, La Crosse, WI, Dublin, Ireland, and possibly dozens of other locations worldwide, communion rails are returning for the first time in half a century. In Santiago, Chile, adoration of the Real Presence reemerged in one of the city's churches after a fifty-year absence. In Liege, Belgium, the newly appointed bishop celebrated the immemorial Mass of all ages. Indeed, all around the globe, a steadily increasing number of Traditional Latin Masses appear with every passing month.

One way or another, reverent Communion on the tongue while kneeling is gaining advocates, despite the rigors and protestations of neo-modernists.

As encouraging as these events might be, they impact just a fraction of the Church. The issues identified within these pages have decimated our ranks and still threaten us, pointed directly at the heart and soul of Roman Catholicism.

In the midst of our present eucharistic storm, without the teaching of transubstantiation, there is no Real Presence. Without the Real Presence, there is little difference between Roman Catholicism and 35,000 Protestant sects, in which case we can all "eat and drink in memory of the Lord's Supper." Without the Real Presence, we have no Holy Eucharist. And without the Holy Eucharist—without adoration, veneration, and reverence, all intrinsically due to the Bread of Life—there is little Catholic identity and no hope of survival.

The Roman Catholic Church, the one true Church of the Holy Eucharist founded by God Himself, is at a critical juncture. All across the Western world, churches are emptying out, closing down, or consolidating. Many parishes are sparsely populated, often almost exclusively by senior citizens. How will these churches look ten years from now? How about twenty years? Will their doors still be open? No one knows, but it is less than promising that entire generations of younger Roman Catholics have been lost, an unmitigated disaster that quietly continues, unrelentingly.

Is there any doubt that the Church is experiencing a crisis? Here are the results from a recent U.S. poll, compliments of Russell Shaw at Catholic World Report:

> Among the 19 percent of Catholics who described themselves as 'committed' in their adherence to the faith, 49 percent said it isn't necessary for a 'good' Catholic to go to Mass weekly, 60 percent said good Catholics needn't follow Church teaching on birth control, 46 percent said the same about the teaching on divorce and remarriage, 31 percent about the teaching on abortion, and 48 percent about marrying in the Church. A surprising 39 percent even said good Catholics needn't give time or money to help the poor. To repeat: these are Catholics who think they're committed in their faith.[1]

The Catherine of Siena Institute in Colorado Springs, CO, has interviewed tens of thousands of Catholics and their pastors and makes this point: "Even among the minority of Catholics who come to Church somewhat regularly, fewer than 10 percent could be considered 'intentional disciples' who have consciously made Christ the center of their lives."[2]

These are the unequivocal results of a global eucharistic storm that has raged on for close to half a century. Its highest, most visible symbol is irreverent Communion in the hand. This cannot be surprising when one considers that fifty percent of Roman Catholics are unaware of the Church's teaching on the Real Presence.[3]

Just as frightening, the current epic collapse is sanctioned by almost universal denial at every level of the Church, and more often than not by utter silence. Since there is no recognized crisis, there is nothing to fix. This is the classic formula for systemic failure.

The wondrous and miraculous gift of the Blessed Sacrament demands and deserves all the protection the Church can possibly muster, and always has. Without an on-going, earnest commitment to protect the Bread of Life, initiated by the Vatican and promoted in every parish worldwide; without resurrecting transubstantiation and the Real Presence, and teaching their redemptive values to every Roman Catholic; and without a return to adoration, veneration, and reverence, a continuing exodus of uncatechized souls is guaranteed.

Yet hope, never far away, beckons. A return to reverence, someday, is inevitable. Progressives are dying out in record numbers. Traditional Catholic churches are flourishing, and traditional seminaries have waiting lists. Moreover, Novus Ordo Catholics, especially younger ones, are awakening to the bitter fruits of Vatican II revisionism. These faithful souls are turning away from modernism and all of its illusionary, destructive veils in a valiant search for truth, honesty, goodness, and beauty.

Where to look? Here are the inspiring words of Pope Saint John Paul II, writing in his last encyclical *Ecclesia de Eucharistia*:

> By giving the Eucharist the prominence it deserves, and by being careful not to diminish any of its dimensions or demands, we

> show that we are truly conscious of the greatness of this gift. We are urged to do so by an uninterrupted tradition, which from the first centuries on has found the Christian community ever vigilant in guarding this "treasure." Inspired by love, the Church is anxious to hand on to future generations of Christians, without loss, her faith and teaching with regard to the mystery of the Eucharist. There can be no danger of excess in our care for this mystery, for "in this sacrament is recapitulated the whole mystery of our salvation."[4]

To a tangible degree, we ignored Pope Saint John Paul II, who argued against the practice on the one hand,[5] but defended it on the other.[6] We spurned His Holiness Pope Benedict XVI, who distributed Communion only to those who knelt, on the tongue, for the final five years of his pontificate (except, as noted earlier, for a small handful of unexplained exceptions).[7] The universal Church simply pretended this breath of fresh air never happened.

Now the weight has passed to Pope Francis I. Will His Holiness accept the challenge, or will the protagonist be an unknown successor?

Just as it happened at Rouen in 650 AD, Communion in the hand will ultimately be condemned by the Church. The innovation of Extraordinary Ministers of Holy Communion, the way we know and experience it today, will be substantially modified. Both transubstantiation and the Real Presence will once again return to their former glory at the heart of Roman Catholicism. This present eucharistic storm will dissipate until it is merely a shadow of its former self.

There will be little choice, for the Church's downward trajectory necessitates a return to traditional Catholic beliefs and practices. At some point, too many lights of the world's Catholic churches will go dark. That event is happening now.

When the day finally dawns and Communion in the hand is abolished, we can count on great protests everywhere. A newly formed storm center will once again break over the Church, led by progressives around the world. Pew sitters will be cajoled and motivated to complain loudly and bitterly.

Neo-modernists are heavily invested in the irreverent practice, and always have been. They birthed, nourished, and disseminated the irreverence to the four corners of the earth. They forced Communion in the hand while standing on a Church that never wanted or sought it, and they will fight to the bitter end to maintain the practice. Despite the obvious damage to the Church, visible to anyone with the will to look, neo-modernists have always refused to acknowledge objective reality, and always will.

It was, in fact, neo-modernists who labored day and night to turn the world's greatest gift—the sacred sacrament of the Bread of Life—into a simple meal. No transubstantiation, no Real Presence, no confession to remove the stain of mortal sin, no reverence, little sacrifice, rampant unbelief—just a nice, Protestant, one-church, "symbolic" meal, frequently received in the hand while standing, often from an EMHC who shouldn't even be there.

What if there is no reversal? What if the practice continues on for another decade or two? Look to Holland for the answers. It was there that irreverent Communion in the hand was birthed in disobedience in the 1960s. Since the closing of the Second Vatican Council, the Dutch bishops have been known as some of the most liberal in the world, leading a global charge away from the Church's traditional emphasis on moral and ecclesiological doctrine and discipline. (The Dutch Catechism, released in 1966 and published worldwide, was a controversial disaster.) Today, *less* than 3 percent of Dutch Catholics regularly attend Sunday Mass—roughly 100,000 out of more than 4 million.[8] On average, two Dutch Catholic churches permanently close and lock their doors *every week*.

Years ago, then-Cardinal Joseph Ratzinger remarked on the strange phenomenon he observed in the post-Vatican II Church of the Netherlands. He pointed out that, by every statistical measure, the Dutch Church was collapsing and yet, strangely, at the same time, an atmosphere of "general optimism" was prevalent. People seemed blind to the actual situation. They didn't seem to care.[9]

Just as irreverent Communion in the hand seamlessly crossed borders in the 1960s, so did the phenomenon first noted by Ratzinger. To one degree or another, the collapse he witnessed in the Netherlands is now worldwide—certainly not as steep, but deep and dramatic nonetheless.

The future Pope Benedict XVI noted the universal danger in 1969 when he wrote,

> The Church will become small and will have to start afresh more or less from the beginning. She will no longer be able to inhabit many of the edifices she built in prosperity. As the number of her adherents diminishes . . . she will lose many of her social privileges.
>
> It will be hard-going for the Church, for the process of crystallization and clarification will cost her much valuable energy. It will make her poor and cause her to become the Church of the meek. . . . The process will be long and wearisome as was the road from the false progressivism on the eve of the French Revolution—when a bishop might be thought smart if he made fun of dogmas and even insinuated that the existence of God was by no means certain. . . .[10]

The innovative experiment of Communion in the hand, a highly visible denial of transubstantiation and the Real Presence, was frighteningly successful. The irreverent practice contributed its fair share to millions of Roman Catholics who walked away from the Church, and continue to do so today. This, the greatest community mass-desertion the world has ever witnessed, is spiritual suicide on an unimaginable scale. Few—very few—of those who deserted had ever been taught what Early Christians were willing to die for.

We cannot survive without the Eucharist. The eucharistic celebration cannot be superseded.

The Eucharist is "the source and summit of the Christian life. The other sacraments, and indeed, all ecclesiastical ministries and works of the apostolate, are bound up with the Eucharist and are oriented toward it. For in the blessed Eucharist is contained the whole spiritual good of the Church, namely Christ himself, our Pasch."[11]

For one to be an intentional disciple of Christ in the Roman Catholic Church, any willful co-existence with irreverence is all but impossible. Eliminating Communion in the hand and restoring the universal Latin Rite of Communion on the tongue while kneeling will restore a sense of the sacred among the faithful, and safeguard the Eucharist from ongoing abuse . . . or worse. Curbing the worldwide innovation of unnecessary EMHCs will send a strong, clear message of unequivocal reverence to Catholics all around the world.

Nothing could be simpler: Those who truly understand and love the Real Presence will rarely, if ever, walk away from the Church of the Holy Eucharist, the one and only custodian of Christ's Body and Blood. Those few who truly understand but still desert will, in all probability, return.

Father Thomas J. McGovern, in his wonderful book *The Most Holy Eucharist*, writes about J. R. R. Tolkien, reflecting on a period when he nearly ceased practicing the Faith. Tolkien intimates how he was rescued by "the never-ceasing, silent appeal of the Tabernacle, and the sense of starving hunger." Writing to his son Michael about marriage, Tolkien, in a revealing account of his own soul, advises him:

> Out of the darkness of my life, so much frustrated, I put before you the one great thing to love on earth: the Blessed Sacrament. . . . There you will find romance, glory, honor, fidelity, and the true way of all your loves on earth, and more than that: Death; by the divine paradox, that which ends life, and demands the surrender of all, and yet by the taste (or foretaste) of which alone can what you seek in your earthly relationships (love, faithfulness, joy) be maintained, or take on that complexion of reality, of eternal endurance, which every man's heart desires.[12]

Tolkien's deep love of the Real Presence was the foundation of his faith, which taught him to receive reverently on the tongue while kneeling before his Savior.

Today, the wide swath of destruction spanning close to half a century is already slowing, the prevailing winds assuaged by a dawning recovery of reverence. How much longer will it be before the storm expires? No one knows, but that day can't come fast enough for the souls of millions of loyal, faithful Catholics, and millions more who will return or convert to the only one true Church of the Holy Eucharist. Here, where we are no longer too proud to humble ourselves, denial, disbelief, confusion, and indifferentism will gradually evaporate over time.

Then, and only then, will the on-going crisis and collapse finally draw toward a close. Only then will we experience the new "spring-time" that has been promised so often, for so long, by so many.

While we pray and expectantly await a universal return to reverence, each of us can receive worthily, on the tongue, and—wherever possible—by kneeling.

Nothing, and no one, should stand in our way.

1 Russell Shaw, "Protocols and Theologians," *Catholic World Report*, August 26, 2012. When this post appeared on communion-in-the-hand.org in September 2013, more than 10,000 people viewed it. Most people who responded appeared to be shell shocked, which makes sense in an era of denial.

2 Ralph Martin, "The Post-Christendom Sacramental Crisis: The Wisdom of Thomas Aquinas," *Nova et Vetera* 11, no. 1 (2013): 57–75. http://www.renewalministries.net/files/freeliterature/novaetvetera11_1martin_(2).pdf.

3 Mary Gautier, "Knowledge and Belief About the Real Presence," *National Catholic Reporter*, http://ncronline.org/news/catholics-america/knowledge-and-belief-about-real-presence.

4 Pope Saint John Paul II, *Ecclesia de Eucharistia*, no. 61, http://www.vatican.va/holy_father/special_features/encyclicals/documents/hf_jp-ii_enc_20030417_ecclesia_eucharistia_en.html. A few years later, after the death of Paul VI, a journalist asked John Paul II what his opinion was in reference to Communion in the hand. The Pope responded, "There is an apostolic letter on the existence of a special valid permission for this. But I tell you that I am not in favor of this practice, nor do I recommend it.

The permission was granted due to the insistence of some diocesan bishops." This took place during an interview by the *Stimme des glaubens* magazine during his visit to Fulda, Germany, in November 1980, as reported in Laise, *Communion in the Hand.*

5 Pope Saint John Paul II in *Dominicae Cenae* wrote:
In some countries, the practice of receiving Communion in the hand has been introduced. This practice has been requested by individual episcopal conferences and has received approval from the Apostolic See. However, cases of a deplorable lack of respect towards the eucharistic species have been reported, cases which are imputable not only to the individuals guilty of such behavior but also to the pastors of the church who have not been vigilant enough regarding the attitude of the faithful towards the Eucharist. It also happens, on occasion, that the free choice of those who prefer to continue the practice of receiving the Eucharist on the tongue is not taken into account in those places where the distribution of Communion in the hand has been authorized. It is therefore difficult in the context of this present letter not to mention the sad phenomena previously referred to. *This is in no way meant to refer to those who, receiving the Lord Jesus in the hand, do so with profound reverence and devotion, in those countries where this practice has been authorized.*" (emphasis added)
See http://www.vatican.va/holy_father/john_paul_ii/letters/documents/hf_jp-ii_let_24021980_dominicae-cenae_en.html.

6 Benedict also wrote that he had no trouble with *reverent* Communion in the hand. Joseph Ratzinger, *God and the World: A Conversation with Peter Seewald* (San Francisco: Ignatius Press, 2002), 410.

7 Benedict distributed Communion in the hand to four or five communicants, and there was never an explanation why from the Vatican.

8 Michael Voris, "Beyond Belief," May 13, 2013, http://www.churchmilitant.tv/daily/?today=2013-05-13.

9 Ratzinger, *God and the World,* 3–40.

10 Joseph Ratzinger, *Faith and the Future* (San Francisco: Ignatius Press, 2009).

11 *Catechism of the Catholic Church*, no. 1324, http://www.usccb.org/beliefs-and-teachings/what-we-believe/catechism/catechism-of-the-catholic-church/epub/index.cfm#.

12 McGovern, *The Most Holy Eucharist,* 119–120.

BIBLIOGRAPHY

Amos, N. Scott. "Martin Bucer and the Revision of the 1549 Book of Common Prayer: Reform of Ceremonies and the Didactic Use of Ritual." *Reformation & Renaissance Review* 2 (1999): 118. http://www.martins-vianna.net/artigos/it3/BUCER_AND_ENGLISH_BOOK_OF_PRAYER.pdf.

"The Articles of Religion: Book of Common Prayer." http://justus.anglican.org/resources/bcp/1928/Articles.htm.

Bernardin, Joseph. "A Consistent Ethic of Life: An American-Catholic Dialogue." Lecture. Fordham University, December 6, 1983. http://www.hnp.org/publications/hnpfocus/BConsistentEthic1983.pdf.

"Bishop Blanchette: A Clear Call for Obedience." National Catholic Register, June 12, 1977.

———. *Ecclesia de Eucharistia.* http://www.vatican.va/holy_father/special_features/encyclicals/documents/hf_jp-ii_enc_20030417_ecclesia_eucharistia_en.html

The Book of Common Prayer and the Holy Bible. New York: Church Publishing, 2007.

Bruns, H. T., ed. *Canones Apostolorum et Conciliorum saeculorum.* Vol. 2. Charleston, SC: Nabu Press, 2011.

Burrus, Virginia. *The Making of a Heretic: Gender, Authority, and the Priscillianist Controversy.* Berkeley, CA: University of California Press, 1995.

Catechism of the Catholic Church. http://www.usccb.org/beliefs-and-teachings/what-we-believe/catechism/catechism-of-the-catholic-church/epub/index.cfm.

Congregation for Divine Worship and the Discipline of the Sacraments. *Redemptionis Sacramentum*. http://www.vatican.va/roman_curia/congregations/ccdds/documents/rc_con_ccdds_doc_20040423_redemptionis-sacramentum_en.html.

Conley, James D. "The Manner of Receiving Holy Communion." *Catholic News Agency*. http://www.catholicnewsagency.com/resources/roman-missal-3rd-edition/bishops/the-manner-of-receiving-holy-communion.

Council of Trent. Session XIII. *Decree Concerning the Most Holy Sacrament of the Eucharist*. http://www.ewtn.com/library/COUNCILS/TRENT13.HTM.

Cyril of Jerusalem. *Catechesis Mystagogica*. In *Patrologia Graeco-Latina*, edited by Jacques-Paul Migne, 33. Paris: Garnier Fratres, 1857–64.

Davies, Michael. *Pope Paul's New Mass.* Kansas City, MO: Angelus Press, 1980.

De Journel, M. J. Rouët. *Enchiridion Patristicum.* Barcelona: Editorial Herder, 1956.

The Didache. http://thedidache.com.

Eusebius. *Ecclesiastical History*. http://www.newadvent.org/fathers/250105.htm.

Fortescue, Adrian. *The Mass: A Study in the Roman Liturgy.* Fitzwilliam, NH: Loreto, 2012.

"Homilies" 4, 4 ca.. 350 AD, Ephrem of Syria: http://www.orthodox-christianity.com/2012/08/early-church-fathers-on-the-eucharist/

Hull, Geoffrey. *The Banished Heart: Origins of Heteropraxis in the Catholic Church.* London: Bloomsbury/T&T Clark, 2010.

Jeroslav Pelikan, *Emergence Of The Catholic Tradition: 100-600, Volume One – The Christian Tradition: A History of the Development of Doctrine* University of Chicago, 1975

Johnston, Francis. *Fatima: The Great Sign.* Charlotte, NC: Tan Books, 1980.

Jungmann, Josef A., S.J. *The Early Liturgy: To the Time of Gregory the Great.* Notre Dame, IN: University of Notre Dame Press, 1959.

Kennedy, Eugene. *Cardinal Bernardin: Easing Conflicts—and Battling for the Soul of American Catholicism.* Los Angeles: Bonus Books, 1989.

Kucharek, Casimir. *The Byzantine-Slav Liturgy of St. John Chrysostom.* Allendale, NJ: Alleluia Press, 1973.

———. *The Sacramental Mysteries: A Byzantine Approach.* Allendale, NJ: Alleluia Press, 1976.

Laise, Juan Rodolfo. *Communion in the Hand: Documents and History.* Boonville, NY: Preserving Christian Publications, 1997.

Letter of the Consilium to Bernard Cardinal Alfrink, Archbishop of Utrecht, Netherlands. October 12, 1965.

Martin, Ralph. "The Post-Christendom Sacramental Crisis: The Wisdom of Thomas Aquinas." *Nova et Vetera* 11, no. 1 (2013): 57–75. http://www.renewalministries.net/files/freeliterature/novaetvetera11_1martin_%282%29.pdf.

McGovern, Thomas J. *The Most Holy Eucharist.* Manchester, NH: Sophia Institute Press, 2013.

Moran, Patrick Francis, *Historical Sketch of the Persecutions Suffered by the Catholics of Ireland Under the Rule of Oliver Cromwell* (Dublin: Callan, 1903).

M. O. W. Oliphant, *Memoir of Count De Montalembert,* (Edinburg and London, William Blackwood and Sons, 1872)Mueller, Mary Magdeleine, OSF, trans., *The Fathers of the Church: St. Caesarius*, Vol. 66 (Washington, DC: Catholic University of America Press, 2004).

National Conference of Catholic Bishops. General Meeting: Minutes. May 3–5, 1977.

Office for the Liturgical Celebrations of the Supreme Pontiff. "Communion Received on the Tongue and While Kneeling." http://www.vatican.va/news_services/liturgy/details/ns_lit_doc_20091117_comunione_en.html.

Origen. *Contra Celsum.* In *Patrologia Graeco-Latina*, edited by Jacques-Paul Migne, vol. 11. Paris: Garnier Fratres, 1857–64.

L'Osservatore Romano, March 19, 1965.

———, June 26, 2008.

———, April 11, 2013.

"Paul VI Saw Liturgical Abuse As Smoke of Satan." *CatholicCulture.org.* http://www.catholicculture.org/news/features/index.cfm?recnum=58473.

Pope Benedict XVI. General Audience. June 27, 2007.

Pope Saint John Paul II. *Dominicae Cenae.* http://www.vatican.va/holy_father/john_paul_ii/letters/documents/hf_jp-ii_let_24021980_dominicae-cenae_en.html.

Pope St. Pius X. *Pascendi Dominici Gregis*. Sept. 8, 1907. http://www.vatican.va/holy_father/pius_x/encyclicals/documents/hf_p-x_enc_19070908_pascendi-dominici-gregis_en.html.

"Pope Warns Against 'Clericalising' the Laity." *Catholic News*, September 25, 2002. http://cathnews.acu.edu.au/209/146.php.

Quasten, Johannes. *Patrology: The Golden Age of Greek Patristic Literature*. Vol. III. Notre Dame, IN: Ave Maria Press, 1950.

Ratzinger, Joseph. "Cardinal Ratzinger's Remarks Regarding the Lefebvre Schism." http://www.catholicculture.org/culture/library/view.cfm?recnum=3032.

———. *Faith and the Future.* San Francisco: Ignatius Press, 2009.

———. *The Spirit of the Liturgy.* San Francisco: Ignatius Press, 2000.

"The Real Presence of Christ in the Eucharist." *The Catholic Encyclopedia*. http://www.newadvent.org/cathen/05573a.htm.

Roach, Larry. "What Modernists (and Neo-modernists) Believe—Pt. 1." *A Blog for Dallas Area Catholics.* http://veneremurcernui.wordpress.com/2013/10/09/what-modernists-and-neo-modernists-believe-pt-1.

Sacred Congregation for Divine Worship. *Memoriale Domini: Instruction on the Manner of Receiving Holy Communion.* May 29, 1969. http://www.ewtn.com/library/curia/cdwmemor.htm.

Sacred Congregation for Divine Worship. *Sacramentali Communione*. http://www.ewtn.com/library/CURIA/CDWBOTH.HTM.

Sacred Congregation of the Sacraments. *Immensae Caritatis*. http://www.ewtn.com/library/CURIA/CDWIMCAR.htm.

St. Gregory Nazianzen. *Oration*. http://www.newadvent.org/fathers/310221.htm.

St. John of Damascus. *De fide Orthodoxa IV*. In *Patrologia Graeco-Latina*, edited by Jacques-Paul Migne, 94. Paris: Garnier Fratres, 1857–64.

Schaff, Philip, *Nicene and Post-Nicene Fathers: First Series, Vol XII: St. Chrysostom: Homilies on the Epistles of Paul to the Corinthians* (New York: Cosimo Classics, 2007).

Schaff, Philip, ed. *A Select library of Nicene and post-Nicene Fathers of the Christian Church.* Grand Rapids, MI: Eerdmans Publishing Company, 1988.

Schneider, Athanasius. *Dominus Est—It Is The Lord! Reflections of a Bishop of Central Asia on Holy Communion.* Pine Beach, NJ: Newman House Press, 2009.

Second Vatican Council. *Sacrosanctum Concilium*. http://www.vatican.va/archive/hist_councils/ii_vatican_council/documents/vat-ii_const_19631204_sacrosanctum-concilium_en.html.

Seewald, Peter. *Light of the World: The Pope, the Church, and the Signs of the Times.* San Francisco: Ignatius Press, 2010.

Shaw, Russell. "Protocols and Theologians." *Catholic World Report*, August 26, 2012. http://www.catholicworldreport.com/Item/1553/protocols_and_theologians.aspx#.

Taouk, Raymond. "Modernism—A Catholic Refutation." http://www.catholicapologetics.info/modernproblems/modernism/modnsm.htm.

Telfer, William. *Cyril of Jerusalem and Nemesius of Emesa.* Louisville, KY: Westminster John Knox Press, 1955.

Theodoret of Cyrrhus. *Canticum Canticorum interpretatio.* In *Patrologia Graeco-Latina*, edited by Jacques-Paul Migne, 81. Paris: Garnier Fratres, 1857–64.

Tisserant, E. "L'Eglise nestorienne." *Dictionnaire de la theologie catholique,* t. XI, col 315. In Laise, *Communion in the Hand: Documents and History*. Boonville, NY: Preserving Christian Publications, 1997.

Voris, Michael. "Beyond Belief." Video, May 13, 2013. http://www.churchmilitant.tv/daily/?today=2013-05-13.

Voris, Michael. “Deliberately Unclear.” Video, June 3, 2013. http://www.youtube.com/watch?v=JFJEUcJ3TOA.

Voris, Michael. “The Most Reverend Bishop Athanasius Schneider: ‘Vatican II Must Be Clarified.’” Interview, June 27, 2013. http://www.youtube.com/watch?v=z8iBeaGeuxw.

Weigel, George. “The End of the Bernardin Era: The Rise, Dominance, and Decline of a Culturally Accommodating Catholicism.” *First Things*, February 2011. http://www.firstthings.com/article/2011/01/the-end-of-the-bernardin-era.

Martin Bucer and the Book of Common Prayer. Great Wakering, UK: Mayhew-McCrimmon, 1974.

Wybrew, Hugh. *The Development of the Eucharistic Liturgy in the Byzantine Rite.* Crestwood, NY: St. Vladimir’s Seminary Press, 1989.

———. *The Orthodox Liturgy.* Yonkers, NY: St. Vladimer’s Seminary Press, 1996.

Zuhlsdorf, John. “Communion in the Hand and the Threat of Death.” *Fr. Z’s Blog.* http://wdtprs.com/blog/2006/06/communion-in-the-hand-and-the-threat-of-death.

MEMORIALE DOMINI

Instruction on the Manner of Distributing Holy Communion – Sacred Congregation for Divine Worship

Issued on May 29, 1969.

When the Church celebrates the memorial of the Lord it affirms by the very rite itself its faith in Christ and its adoration of him, Christ present in the sacrifice and given as food to those who share the eucharistic table.

For this reason it is a matter of great concern to the Church that the Eucharist be celebrated and shared with the greatest dignity and fruitfulness. It preserves intact the already developed tradition which has come down to us, its riches having passed into the usage and the life of the Church The pages of history show that the celebration and the receptions of the Eucharist have taken various forms. In our own day the rites for the celebration of the Eucharist have been changed in many and important ways, bringing them more into line with modern man's spiritual and psychological needs. Further, a change has taken place in the discipline governing the laity's participation in the sacrament. Holy communion under two kinds, bread and wine has been reintroduced. It had once been common in the Latin Church too, but had subsequently been progressively abandoned. This state of affairs had become general by the time of the Council of Trent, which sanctioned and defended it by dogmatic teaching as being suited to the conditions of that time.[clii]

These changes have made of the eucharistic banquet and the faithful fulfillment of Christ's command a clearer and more vital symbol. At the same time in recent years a fuller sharing in the eucharistic celebration through sacramental communion has here and there evoked the desire to return to the ancient usage of depositing the eucharistic bread in the hand of the communicant, he himself then communicating, placing it in his mouth.

Indeed, in certain communities and in certain places this practice has been introduced without prior approval having been requested of the Holy See, and, at times, without any attempt to prepare the faithful adequately.

It is certainly true that ancient usage once allowed the faithful to take this divine food in their hands and to place it in their mouths themselves.

It is also true that in very ancient times they were allowed to take the Blessed Sacrament with them from the place where the holy sacrifice was celebrated. This was principally so as to be able to give themselves Viaticum in case they had to face death for their faith.

However, the Church's prescriptions and the evidence of the Fathers make it abundantly clear that the greatest reverence was shown the Blessed Sacrament, and that people acted with the greatest prudence. Thus, "let nobody . . . eat that flesh without first adoring it."[cliii] As a person takes (the Blessed Sacrament) he is warned: ". . . receive it: be careful lest you lose any of it."[cliv] "For it is the Body of Christ."[clv]

Further, the care and the ministry of the Body and Blood of Christ was specially committed to sacred ministers or to men specially designated for this purpose: "When the president has recited the prayers and all the people have uttered an acclamation, those whom we call deacons distribute to all those present the bread and wine for which thanks have been given, and they take them to those who are absent."[clvi]

Soon the task of taking the Blessed Eucharist to those absent was confided to the sacred ministers alone, so as the better to ensure the respect due to the sacrament and to meet the needs of the faithful. Later, with a deepening understanding of the truth of the eucharistic mystery, of its power and of the presence of Christ in it, there came a greater feeling of reverence towards this sacrament and a deeper humility was felt to be demanded when receiving it. Thus the custom was established of the minister placing a particle of consecrated bread on the tongue of the communicant.

This method of distributing holy communion must be retained, taking the present situation of the Church in the entire world into account, not merely because it has many centuries of tradition behind it, but especially because it expresses the faithful's reverence for the Eucharist. The custom does not detract in any way from the personal dignity of those who approach this great sacrament: it is part of that preparation that is needed for the most fruitful reception of the Body of the Lord.[clvii]

This reverence shows that it is not a sharing in "ordinary bread and wine"[clviii] that is involved, but in the Body and Blood of the Lord, through which "The people of God share the benefits of the Paschal Sacrifice, renew the New Covenant which God has made with man once for all through the Blood of Christ, and in faith and hope foreshadow and anticipate the eschatological banquet in the kingdom of the Father."[clix]

Further, the practice which must be considered traditional ensures, more effectively, that holy communion is distributed with the proper respect, decorum and dignity. It removes the danger of profanation of the sacred species, in which "in a unique way, Christ, God and man, is present whole and entire, substantially and continually."[clx] Lastly, it ensures that diligent carefulness about the fragments of consecrated bread which the Church has always recommended: "What you have allowed to drop, think of it as though you had lost one of your own members."[clxi]

When therefore a small number of episcopal conferences and some individual bishops asked that the practice of placing the consecrated hosts in the people's hands be permitted in their territories, the Holy Father decided that all the bishops of the Latin Church should be asked if they thought it opportune to introduce this rite. A change in a matter of such moment, based on a most ancient and venerable tradition, does not merely affect discipline. It carries certain dangers with it which may arise from the new manner of administering holy communion: the danger of a loss of reverence for the august sacrament of the altar, of profanation, of adulterating the true doctrine.

Three questions were asked of the bishops, and the replies received by 12 March 1969 were as follows:

1. Do you think that attention should be paid to the desire that, over and above the traditional manner, the rite of receiving holy communion on the hand should be admitted?
   Yes: 597
   No: 1,233
   Yes, but with reservations: 315
   Invalid votes: 20
2. Is it your wish that this new rite be first tried in small communities, with the consent of the bishop?
   Yes: 751
   No: 1,215
   Invalid votes, 70
3. Do you think that the faithful will receive this new rite gladly, after a proper catechetical preparation?
   Yes: 835
   No: 1,185
   Invalid votes: 128

From the returns it is clear that the vast majority of bishops believe that the present discipline should not be changed, and that if it were, the change would be offensive to the sentiments and the spiritual culture of these bishops and of many of the faithful.

Therefore, taking into account the remarks and the advice of those whom "the Holy Spirit has placed to rule over" the Churches,[clxii] in view of the gravity of the matter and the force of the arguments put forward, the Holy Father has decided not to change the existing way of administering holy communion to the faithful.

The Apostolic See therefore emphatically urges bishops, priests and laity to obey carefully the law which is still valid and which has again been confirmed. It urges them to take account of the judgment given by the majority of Catholic bishops, of the rite now in use in the liturgy, of the common good of the Church.

Where a contrary usage, that of placing holy communion on the hand, prevails, the Holy See—wishing to help them fulfill their task, often difficult as it is nowadays—lays on those conferences the task of weighing carefully whatever special circumstances may exist there, taking care to avoid any risk of lack of respect or of false opinions with regard to the Blessed Eucharist, and to avoid any other ill effects that may follow.

In such cases, episcopal conferences should examine matters carefully and should make whatever decisions, by a secret vote and with a two-thirds majority, are needed to regulate matters. Their decisions should be sent to Rome to receive the necessary confirmation,[clxiii] accompanied with a detailed account of the reasons which led them to take those decisions. The Holy See will examine each case carefully, taking into account the links between the different local churches and between each of them and the Universal Church, in order to promote the common good and the edification of all, and that mutual good example may increase faith and piety.

Note: The Instruction was accompanied by a sample of the letter (in French) which is sent to hierarchies who ask for and are granted permission to introduce the practice of holy communion on the hand. The letter laid down the following regulations:[clxiv]

1. The new method of administering communion should not be imposed in a way that would exclude the traditional usage. . . .

2. The rite of communion in the hand must be introduced tactfully. In effect, since human attitudes are in question, it is linked with the sensibility of the person receiving communion. It should therefore be introduced gradually, beginning with better-educated and better-prepared groups. It is, above all, necessary that an adequate catechesis prepares the way so that the faithful will understand the significance of the action and will perform it with the respect due to the sacrament. The result of this catechesis should be to remove any suggestion of wavering on the part of the Church in its faith in the eucharistic presence, and also to remove any danger or even suggestion of profanation.

3. The fact that the lay person is now able to receive holy communion in the hand should not suggest to him that this is ordinary bread, or just any sacred object. Rather ought it to strengthen his sense of his dignity as a member of the Mystical Body of Christ, of which baptism and the grace of the Eucharist make him a part. He will thus experience an increase of faith in the great reality of the Body and Blood of the Lord which he touches with his hands. His respectful attitude should be proportionate to what he is doing.

4. With regard to the manner of administering the sacrament, one may follow the traditional method, which emphasized the ministerial function of the priest or deacon, in having them place the host in the hand of the communicant. One may also adopt a simpler method, allowing the communicant himself to take the host from the ciborium. In either case, the communicant ought to consume the host before returning to his place, and the minister's role will be emphasized by his saying, "The Body of Christ," to which the communicant responds, "Amen."

5. No matter which method is adopted, one will be careful not to allow any fragment of the host to fall. . . .

6. When the communion is distributed under both kinds, it is never permitted to place in the hands of the communicants hosts which have first been placed in the Blood of the Lord.

7. Bishops who have been permitted to introduce the new rite of communion are asked to send a report to the congregation, six months hence, on the outcome.

clii Cf. Council of Trent, session 21, The Doctrine of Communion under Both Kinds: *Denz.* 1726–1727.
cliii St. Augustine, *On the Psalms*, 98, 9.
cliv St. Cyril of Jerusalem, *Mystagogic Catechesis*, V, 21.
clv Hippolytus, *Apostolic Tradition*, no. 37.
clvi Justin, *Apologia*, 1, 65.
clvii See St. Augustine, *On the Psalms*, 98, 9.
clviii See Justin, *Apologia*, 1, 66.
clix Instruction *Eucharisticum Mysterium*, no. 3.
clx *Ibid.*, no. 9.
clxi St. Cyril of Jerusalem, *Mystagogic Catechesis*, V, 21.
clxii See Acts 20:28.
clxiii See Vatican II Decree *Christus Dominus*, no. 38, par. 4.
clxiv Translated by Rev. Austin Flannery, O.P., *Acta Apostolicae Sedis* 61 (1969), 541–47.

Made in the USA
Coppell, TX
16 December 2020